MUSEO DEL PRADO  Guide

Mar Sánchez Ramón

EDICIONES
Aldeasa

HISTORY OF THE MUSEUM

The Prado Museum first opened on 19 November 1819, when it had the name of the Royal Museum of Painting and Sculpture, in reference to the fact that the works of art came from the collections of the Spanish monarchs. In 1872 the collection was expanded with the arrival of works of art from the controversial Museo de la Trinidad, set up through Mendizábal's Law of Disentailment (*Ley de Desamortización*) of 1836, following the seizure of works of art formerly owned by the monasteries in Spain. The new museum would be one of the first to follow the French model of the Musée du Louvre (opened in 1793), whose main feature — other than its public character which resulted from the nationalisation of the country's artistic heritage, previously in the hands of the ruling classes — was its educational and recreational function.

The four years between 1814, when Ferdinand VII explicitly stated his wish to create a museum of painting, and the date of its opening, were devoted to the search for an ideal site for displaying the collection. Eventually, in 1818, the Royal Museum of Natural Sciences was selected. The building was part of Charles III's splendid project to create an Academy of Natural Sciences situated in the part of Madrid which he had chosen to develop: the Prado de San Jerónimo. The building, designed by Juan de Villanueva and built between 1785 and 1808 in a fine Neo–classical style, consisted of three large elements joined by long galleries which offered the perfect setting for showing paintings from the royal collection. However, the fabric of the building had been seriously damaged during the Peninsular Wars and a campaign of restoration was undertaken, initially by Villanueva himself then, after his death, by Antonio López Aguado: following his intervention, the building was ready for opening in 1819. Since then, the Prado Museum has continued to grow and adapt itself to the necessities of the age. Important alterations to the building include, in chronological order, those of Narciso Pascual y Colomer, who designed the basilica and apse of the central element (1853); Francisco Jarreño, who added a monumental stairway to the north façade and opened windows onto the lower floor (1882 and 1885); in 1927, Arbó planned to enlarge the rooms on the back part of the building; around the mid–century Pedro de Muguruza redesigned the central gallery and added a new stairwell to the north part (which was heavily criticised as it destroyed the splendid staircase designed by Jarreño) with the aim of introducing more light into the crypt area; while Chueca and Lorente both expanded the galleries (1956 and 1967). In 1971 the Museum was expanded by the addition of the Casón del Buen Retiro to house the nineteenth– and twentieth–century paintings. At the present time, work has begun on an expansion project designed by Rafael Moneo. This will not involve major changes to Villanueva's building, which will gain additional space for the services and amenities required in any modern museum, and will be completed in the next few years.

View of the Royal Museum of Painting, Madrid, ca. 1820.
Lithograph based on a painting by F. Brambilla

Ground Floor

SAN BAUDELIO DE BERLANGA
The Deer Hunt, 185 x 246 cm.
Elephant, 205 x 136 cm.
(1) *Soldier or Hunter,* 290 x 134 cm.
(2) *Bear,* 202 x 113 cm.
(3) *Hare Hunt,* 185 x 360 cm.
Curtain decorated with Wheels and Eagles, 155 x 114 cm.
Wall painting transferred to canvas
REF. NOS. 7263 TO 7268

These paintings were acquired through an exchange with the Metropolitan Museum, New York, and are the oldest in the Prado's collection. They are exceptional both for the subject matter, which is secular at a time when most art was religious (and even more unusual as they were painted for the walls of a church) and also for the realistic style of representation.

The paintings were originally murals, but were transferred to canvas so that they could be removed from their original location and sold outside Spain. They come from the Mozarabic church (Mozarabic meaning made by Christian craftsmen in territory ruled over by the Arabs in Spain) of San Baudelio de Berlanga in the province of Soria. The group consists of six subjects depicting a *Deer Hunt,* an *Elephant,* a *Soldier* or *Hunter,* a *Bear,* a *Hare Hunt,* and a *Curtain decorated with Wheels and Eagles* (the last based on Eastern iconography). The reasons for painting these subjects are unknown, but it has been suggested that the church may have functioned as a hunting retreat for the kings of Leon, during which time its walls were painted with hunting subjects, and that it later returned to its religious function.

With regard to the realistic style, the clothing of the figures has been compared with Mozarabic painting, which has come down to us in all its splendour today in the magnificent manuscripts known as the *Beatos.*

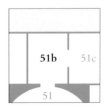

(3)

(1)

(2)

SANTA CRUZ, MADERUELO

(Chapel reconstructed inside the museum)
Wall painting transferred to canvas. 498 x 450 cm.
REF. NOS. 7269 TO 7287

During the Romanesque period, painting is found on the walls and vaults of churches and was primarily used to decorate holy buildings, through the representation and visual explanation of religious subjects. The present paintings decorated the walls of the little church of Santa Cruz in Maderuelo (Segovia), and are particularly interesting in that they are displayed in the Museum as they would have been originally seen. The chapel is of rectangular form with a canon vault and flat end wall. Starting with the main subject, on the vault of the apse is the *Pantocrator*, whose mandorla is supported by angels. On the side walls, divided into two levels are the *Tetramorphs* arranged on both sides on the lower level, and in the upper level there is possibly a Virgin and another unidentified image.

In the upper part of the sanctuary are the *Holy Lamb*, the *Cross*, *Cain and Abel*, the *Magdalen anointing Christ's Feet* and the *Epiphany*. Above the entrance door in the lunettes are depictions of the *Creation of Adam* and of the *Temptation of Eve*. According to the art historian Pérez Sánchez, it is here that we find the most remarkable scenes of the group which reveal an extraordinary command of draughtsmanship and vigorous lines used to execute the nude figures, combined with a refined and decorative treatment of the branches of the trees. The whole is notable for its varied colouring and a crispness of line that creates a uniform style.

These paintings are related to those in the church of Santa María in Tahull, Cataluña, a connection which has been explained by the existence of a series of workshops of painters who travelled around Spain, disseminating a style which was identical in style and approach to the present paintings.

< 51b **51c**   58 >

BARTOLOMÉ BERMEJO (c. 1460–1498)
Saint Domingo of Silos enthroned as Abbot, c. 1475
Painting on panel, 242 x 130 cm.
REF. NO. 1323

Bartolomé de Cárdenas, nicknamed "Bermejo", is the most important of all the Aragonese Gothic artists. He was probably born in Cordoba, but soon moved to the kingdom of Aragon (living in Valencia, and later either Barcelona or Daroca), where he remained for the rest of his life.

This altar painting represents the Bishop of Silos, Saint Domingo, painted on a monumental scale and in a frontal pose, with his mitre, staff and cope and enthroned on a platform within an elaborate Gothic structure with ornate gilded carving. Around the throne are representations of the Virtues, each one within a typically Gothic niche. The bishop's face is painted in a vigorously realistic, almost sculptural style, achieved by the use of very obvious and pronounced strokes. The rest of the space, which is also powerfully realised, is treated in a refined, sculptural manner.

Bermejo executed this work for the church of Santo Domingo de Silos in Daroca (Zaragoza), which was built at around this date. The present painting is one of the finest examples of Aragonese painting now in the collection of the Prado.

< 51   50   49 >

Fra Angelico (ca. 1387–1455)
The Annunciation Altarpiece, ca. 1435
Panel painting, 194 x 194 cm.
Ref. no. 15

The fifteenth century was a time of important reforms in the Church, resulting in a need for a clear and simple mode of representing this new faith. The artist who created this new image was himself a monk of the Dominican Order: Fra Giovanni da Fiesole, or Fra Angelico. A man of his time, he was aware of new developments in painting. In his *Lives of the Artists*, Vasari describes him as carefully studying Masaccio's frescoes in the Brancacci Chapel in Florence, works which heralded the advent of the new Renaissance style. Modern but at the same time conservative, an artist-craftsman and theologian, Fra Angelico is in essence the perfect Dominican, as his work expresses a dialectical rigour and didactic aim.

This simple altarpiece, painted for the Dominican convent in Fiesole uses a type of architectural structure which is already Renaissance in style, reminiscent of the arcading of Brunelleschi's Ospedale degli Innocenti. On the left is a depiction of the *Expulsion from the Garden of Eden*, the principal scene represents the *Annunciation*, while the predella has five scenes from the Life of the Virgin, namely the *Birth* and *Marriage* of the Virgin, the *Visitation*, the *Adoration of the Magi*, the *Purification in the Temple*, and the *Death of the Virgin*. The Virgin's humble and submissive pose indicates that she has already accepted the burden of being the mother of Christ. As the art historian Anthony Blunt noted, when depicting this episode, every artist chooses the moment that corresponds most closely with his own personal convictions.

Fra Angelico's painting emphasises the concreteness of the physical reality of objects, as well as revealing a unity of light, colour and form. All these he used to "give a perfect home to perfect things", coinciding with Dominican thought of the period. Fra Angelico drew on the qualities of the new perception of space in art although he did not necessarily apply it uniformly. For the poet Yves Bonnefoy, "Fra Angelico's true medium was light; an intermediary and ambiguous reality, half physical, half spiritual". His light envelops the object, making it part of the perfection, in line with contemporary Neo–platonic and religious thinking. He avoids contrast and paradox, and everything in the work seems to share in the celestial vision.

SANDRO BOTTICELLI (ca. 1444–1510)
The Story of Nastagio degli Onesti, ca. 1483
Panel painting, approx. 83 x 138 cm. each panel
SCENE I. REF. NO. 2838, SCENE II. REF. NO. 2839, SCENE III. REF. NO. 2840

Alessandro Filipepi, known as Sandro Botticelli, was trained in the workshop of
Filippo Lippi. By the time he painted these panels he was already a mature and fully established artist. Following the wall paintings that he carried out in the Sistine Chapel, he worked
in the service of Lorenzo il Magnifico and for Lorenzo's Neo–platonic Academy. He was also
at this period artistic tutor to Giuliano de' Medici.

These three panels come from a *cassone* or wedding chest commissioned by Antonio
Pucci for the marriage of his son Giannozzo with Lucrezia Bini. The story depicted is one of
the tales in Bocaccio's *Decameron* (Day 5, tale VIII). Nastagio, in love with a young woman,
is walking in a wood in an attempt to restore his peace of mind and to meditate. Suddenly he
comes across a terrible scene: a young girl running away from a rider who catches up with her,
runs her through the heart with his lance and extracts her entrails (Scene I). The same scene
then happens again before his horrified gaze. Nastagio attempts to help the girl but is dis-
suaded by the knight, Guido degli Anastagi, who tells him his story: after his beloved reject-
ed him, he committed suicide, but this failed to move the stony–hearted woman who was
therefore condemned to be pursued by her suitor who would tear out her heart, a punishment
to last as long as the period of her original indifference (Scene II). Nastagio therefore had the
idea of organising a feast in the wood, to which he invited the family of his beloved so that
they could witness the terrible story and draw their own conclusions (Scene III). The result
was a happy one and Nastagio was able to marry his beloved. The Prado series lacks the final
panel, which is in the Watney Collection.

Botticelli's painting is characterised by his perfectly balanced and rhythmical compositions. The present work, which was probably by his studio, lacks his typical representation of
female beauty in the depiction of the main figure in all the scenes, however Botticelli's own
hand is obvious in the painting of the dogs, which are the best elements in the three panels.

ANDREA MANTEGNA (ca. 1431–1506)
The Death of the Virgin, ca. 1460
Panel painting, 54 x 42 cm.
REF. NO. 248

Andrea Mantegna is one of the great figures of Italian Renaissance painting. Born in the Veneto, he was trained in Padua where the university was among the foremost centres of Humanist studies in Europe. There he coincided with Donatello, who was in Padua to work on the equestrian sculpture of the *Condottiero Gattamelata,* and whose work had a profound influence on Mantegna. He later travelled to Rome, where he admired the classical art and architecture which would be strongly reflected in his own work.

Mantegna returned north to Venice, where he married Nicolosia, the daughter of Jacopo Bellini, whose art was a key influence on his own. Mantegna's painting always deployed markedly solid, sculptural forms. In his *Lives of the Artists,* Vasari quotes the artist as saying that sculptures were more perfect than nature.

In 1459 the artist entered the service of the Gonzaga, for whom he painted the present work. The subject has been known by three different names: *The Transition of the Virgin, The Dormition of the Virgin* and the *Death of the Virgin.* According to Christian tradition, after the birth of Christ, the Virgin moved to Ephesus, where the Archangel Gabriel announced to the Virgin her death. She requested the presence of Saint John the Evangelist, who arrived transported on a cloud. The other Apostles were similarly forewarned of the event and arrived to find the Virgin on her deathbed. Mantegna sets the event within a solidly–constructed architectural framework, while the figures are highly sculptural and the composition perfectly resolved through the use of horizontal and vertical lines. In the background is a view of Mantua with the Ponte di San Giorgio between the Middle and Lower lakes.

ANTONELLO DA MESSINA (1430–1479)
The Dead Christ supported by an Angel, ca. 1476
Oil on panel, 74 x 51 cm.
REF. NO. 3092

Antonello was born in the Sicilian city of Messina, and began his artistic training in Naples, travelling from there to Flanders and later to Venice, where he arrived in 1474, bringing with him such important artistic innovations as oil painting, a Flemish technique that would spread from Venetian artistic circles to the rest of Italy. His mature work clearly shows this eclecticism in his training, representing an interesting combination of Italian idealism and Flemish realism, the two major trends within European Renaissance painting.

The present painting, which dates from shortly after his return to Messina, shows his knowledge of idealised Italian painting — indebted to Giovanni Bellini — and northern realism with its interest in conveying every detail with great precision, evident here in the treatment of the landscape or Christ's hair.

The dead Christ is represented with great monumentality and drama, supported by a tearful angel so small that it seems miraculous that it can support Christ's weight. Also notable is the fact that only one angel supports the body, whereas the norm was to represent two in this type of composition. The tragic mood of the scene is counterbalanced by the light and clarity of the daytime sky, which seems to convey the idea of the Resurrection and hence of Man's salvation.

57b

< 50 ▶ **49**

RAPHAEL — RAFFAELLO SANZIO — (1483–1520)

Portrait of a Cardinal, ca. 1510
Panel painting, 79 x 61 cm.
REF. NO. 299

Raphael first studied with his father and later in Perugino's workshop, but it is really in Florence, along with Leonardo and Michelangelo (whose works he studied and absorbed) that he became one of the key figures of the second generation of Renaissance artists. Due to his high reputation, he was called to Rome by Julius II in 1508 and worked there until his death. In Rome he painted the present portrait, which was probably a commission from a Roman cardinal, although the sitter's name is now lost.

The figure of the cardinal in red stands out strongly against the dark background. His quiet pose and almost enigmatic expression conveys the idea of a reserved, even austere man, despite his position as a prince of the Church; we might describe him as a simple man, although distinguished and elegant. Raphael used a very subtle technique, of sombre draughtsmanship and uniform, strong colours. The result is a troubling work, despite its overwhelming sense of realism.

The Prado has an important group of works by Raphael dating from his mature period. Among them are *The Holy Family with the Lamb* (Ref. No. 296, ca. 1504), *The Virgin of the Fish* (Ref. No. 297, ca. 1513), *Christ on the Route to Calvary* (Ref. No. 298, ca. 1517), *The Holy Family*, "The Pearl" (Ref. No. 301, ca. 1518), *The Virgin of the Rose* (Ref. No. 302, ca. 1518), and *The Holy Family of the Oak* (Ref. No. 303, ca. 1518).

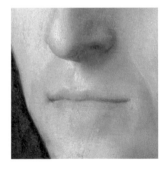

56b	55b

▲

49

ANTONIO ALLEGRI DA CORREGGIO (ca. 1493–1534)
"Noli me tangere", ca. 1520
Panel transferred to canvas, 130 x 103 cm.
REF. NO. 111

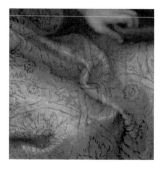

Antonio Allegri was born in Correggio, a small town between Parma and Mantua in northern Italy. His most important works are to be found in Parma, where he was painter to Duke Federico Gonzaga, governor of that city. His working method, which was based on that of the Venetian painters, consisted of working directly onto the canvas, although in the case of Correggio he used preparatory drawings to work out the composition beforehand. His work falls largely within the current of art history described as Mannerism. His painting reflects the influence of Leonardo da Vinci, while at times he made use of Mantegna's innovations with regard to foreshortening and perspective. However, Correggio's overall style is completely unique and his paintings depict mythological subjects of enormous sensuality, to the extent that one could see in this aspect of his work a foretaste of 18th–century Rococo eroticism and sensuality.

The present painting belongs to his most classicising period, at the time when he was painting the interior of the church of San Giovanni in Parma. Christ, dressed as a gardener, appears to Mary Magdalen, who looks at Him with astonishment and admiration. The pallor of Christ's skin, the treatment of his limbs and his complex pose result in a figure which is perhaps slightly weak but has a certain beauty. The use of a blue robe for Christ is novel, as until now artists had depicted Him in colours close to white or tending to pink, while the yellow of the Magdalen's robe was the colour traditionally used to depict prostitutes or adulteresses. Both colours are strong and vivid. The rendering of the light in this painting (considered one of Correggio's masterpieces) is achieved with a perfect sense of harmony.

56b | 55b

49

47 >

Introduction and Development of the New Style in Spain. Castille

Pedro de Berruguete (ca. 1450–1504)
Auto da fé with Saint Dominic of Guzmán, ca. 1490
Panel painting, 154 x 92 cm.
Ref. no. 618

Pedro Berruguete is a key figure in Spanish art as he introduced into Castille the innovations of Renaissance art and subsequently developed them. Around 1475 he was working in Italy for Duke Federico da Montefeltro at the Duke's palace in Urbino, one of the most important artistic centres of the period. In the early 1480s Berruguete returned to Spain.

The present painting depicts an episode in the life of the saint in which he succeeds in obtaining a pardon for some Albigensian heretics. Berruguete constructed a Renaissance-style setting for the painting through a use of rational architecture. However, the highly detailed treatment of the figures, clothed in contemporary dress, falls within the Flemish tradition, as does the narrative approach with its anecdotal elements introduced through the secondary characters. Overall, Berruguete created a unique and personal style through his combination of two totally different trends — the Italian and Flemish — combined with some Hispano–Moresque elements derived from native Spanish art.

Other works by Berruguete in the Prado are *Saint Paul* (Ref. No. 123), *Saint Peter* (Ref. No. 124), *The Adoration of the Magi* (Ref. No. 125), *Two Magi* (Ref. No. 126), *Saint Dominic and the Albigensians* (Ref. No. 609), *Saint Dominic revives a Boy* (Ref. No. 610), *The Sermon of Saint Peter Martyr* (Ref. No. 611), *Saint Peter Martyr at Prayer* (Ref. No. 612), *The Death of Saint Peter Martyr* (Ref. No. 613), *The Tomb of Saint Peter Martyr* (Ref. No. 614), *The Apparition of the Virgin to a Community of Monks* (Ref. No. 615), *Saint Dominic of Guzmán* (Ref. No. 616), *Saint Peter Martyr* (Ref. No. 617), *The Test by Fire* (Ref. No. 1305), *The Virgin and Child* (Ref. No. 2709), and *The Resurrection of Christ* (Ref. No. 3109).

THE RENAISSANCE IN VALENCIA

JUAN DE JUANES — VICENTE JUAN MASIP — (ca. 1523–1579)
The Last Supper, ca. 1560
Painting on canvas, 116 x 191 cm.
REF. NO. 846

Juan de Juanes was the son of Vicente Masip, a notable artist who introduced the High Renaissance style of Raphael into Valencia. The work of Juan de Juanes continues within the line of his father's while retaining some slight Leonardesque elements, toned down by his use of a highly detailed technique with the additional element of a sweet, devotional style which was probably required of him by his patrons. This style made his work enormously popular, and his fame and popularity have lasted to the present day. *The Last Supper* and the series on the Life of Saint Stephen formed part of the high altar of the church of Saint Stephen in Valencia.

The Last Supper is one of Juan de Juanes' most famous works. The compositional arrangement recalls Leonardo's version painted on the walls of Santa Maria delle Grazie in Milan, which Juan would have seen during his Italian trip. Here, however, he emphasises a different moment in the Gospel episode; the blessing of the bread, considered a key episode in the mass at this period. The disposition of Christ, painted beneath an arch with a landscape visible behind, is typical of Leonardo and would be taken up by Italian Mannerist painting. In this painting Juan de Juanes's work reached a peak of perfection: the painting is at once a still life, a devotional icon which depicts a moment of high drama, and to some extent a landscape. While the work is not devoid of a Mannerist theatricality, all the different elements within it are conveyed with a sense of realism.

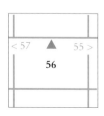

Attributed to
ROGIER VAN DER WEYDEN (ca. 1400–1464)
The Descent from the Cross, ca. 1435
Oil on panel, 220 x 262 cm.
REF. NO. 2825

It was Jan van Eyck, and to an even greater extent, Rogier van der Weyden, whose works established the conventions for Northern European painting until the first decades of the sixteenth century. Van der Weyden was a pupil of Robert Campin, but differs from his style in giving less importance to individual detail, which he subordinates to the overall effect of the composition. This important Flemish painting formed the central panel of a large triptych painted for the Chapel of the Crossbowmen in Louvaine, Belgium. Despite the drama of the scene, the artist uses bright, light colours against a gold background. There are two focuses of attention, Christ and the Virgin; both figures are arranged on a parallel with the Virgin on a lower plane to Christ. According to the art historian Jonathan Brown, the painting contains three episodes compressed into one scene: the Descent from the Cross, the Lamentation over the Dead Christ and the Burial of Christ. The figures, which are highly individualised, each convey their intense grief that overwhelms them. The painter has chosen the moment when Joseph of Arimathaea, Nicodemus and an assistant support Christ's body in the air, while Maria falls almost swooning to the ground, held up by Saint John. The painting is also notable for the use of extremely costly materials, such as the lapis lazuli for the Virgin's robe which is among the most pure ever employed in Flemish painting. The figures, painted life size, are arranged in a shallow space encouraging the spectator to see them as sculpture, although more lifelike than sculpture could be. Other works by Van der Weyden in the Prado include *The Virgin and Child* (Ref. No. 2722, ca. 1435) and *The Pietà* (Ref. No. 2540, ca. 1440).

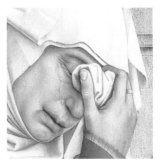

Attributed to
PETRUS CHRISTUS (ca. 1415 – ca. 1472)
The Virgin and Child, ca. 1460
Oil on panel, 59 x 34 cm.
REF. NO. 1921

Petrus Christus (born in Baerle, near Tilburg) is a painter whose work falls within the current of the Flemish painting produced in the city of Bruges. Christus had a profound knowledge of the work of Robert Campin and Rogier van der Weyden: working in the second half of the fifteenth century, he absorbed the lessons of the earlier painters, simplifying the forms and giving them an almost sculptural weight. Christus' religious scenes exude an enormous sense of calm.

His portraits — in this case the face of the Virgin — express the state of mind of the figure represented. Here, the Virgin's thoughtful gaze and her red robe allude to the future suffering and death of her son. The Virgin, acting like a throne to the figure of the Christ Child, is seated with her back to a portico which opens onto a broad, panoramic landscape with a wide river, buildings and trees. An angel is about to crown her. The Christ Child holds up a crystal orb topped by a cross, indicating that He is here represented as Christ the Saviour, while the Virgin is crowned as Queen of the Heavens.

In comparison to Jan van Eyck's analytical approach to painting which aimed to capture even the smallest detail, Petrus Christus simplifies the focus, resulting in a more meditative and intimate mood.

Attributed to
JAN VAN EYCK (1390–1441)
*The Fountain of Grace and the Triumph of the Church
over the Synagogue*, ca. 1440
Oil on panel, 181 x 116 cm.
REF. NO. 1511

The attribution of this panel has been much discussed, although it is generally attributed to Van Eyck, who is also traditionally said to have invented oil painting. The remarkably transparent quality of his application of pigments and the successive overlaying of glazes gave his paintings a jewel–like quality that no reproduction can convey. His ability to convey space rivals the achievements of the most famous of the Italian painters of his day.

The composition is arranged on three levels like a great stage set and suggests the religious performances that were held in Van Eyck's day during holy festivals. The totally symmetrical composition is arranged on a late Gothic architectural structure. In the upper level is God the Father in the centre with the Lamb at His feet, and to either side the Virgin and Saint John as intercessors for Mankind. In the middle level are musical angels in a garden. On the lower, or earthly, level is the fountain in the centre which gives rise to the name of the painting, where we see the Holy Forms; to the right of God (on our left) the Church is represented by figures of different social status such as a pope, a cardinal, a bishop, an abbot, a theologian, an emperor, a king (who has been identified as Philip the Good, Duke of Burgundy, governor of extensive territories in Northern Europe at this period), among others. To our right is the vanquished Synagogue or Jewish religion; a high priest with his eyes blindfolded and a broken staff, and ten jews (identified as such by the Hebrew inscriptions), who are depicted as defeated and in disarray.

HANS MEMLING (ca. 1435–1494)
The Adoration of the Magi, ca. 1470
Triptych on panel, 95 x 63 cm. (wings), 95 x 145 cm. (central panel)
REF. NO. 1557

Hans Memling was the leading artist in Bruges of the generation after Van Eyck. Little is known of his life until around 1465, the year he settled in Bruges, registering himself in the Citizen's Book as a native of Seligenstadt, a small town near Frankfurt where he is thought to have been born around 1435–1440. It is not known whether he trained as a painter in Germany before moving to Flanders. In the mid–fifteenth century at the time Memling was learning to paint, German painting was strongly influenced by Flemish innovations, and it is therefore likely that the young artist would have wanted to go directly to the Low Countries, where he abandoned all the German aspects of his art and became a completely Flemish painter.

One year before Memling's arrival in Bruges, Rogier van der Weyden had died in Brussels, and these two events are probably connected. In his earliest compositions, Memling

uses a technique very close to that of Van der Weyden, and remains faithful throughout his career to a repertoire of motifs and compositions derived from that artist. We might thus conclude that he worked closely with Van der Weyden until the older artist's death obliged him to go his own way, although there is no documentary evidence to prove Memling's stay in Brussels. Whatever the case, it was his reputation as a pupil of Van der Weyden that gained him his first commission.

The present triptych is fairly close to one painted by Van der Weyden for the church of Saint Columba in Cologne (now in the Alte Pinakothek in Munich). Here Memling spreads the figures out so broadly across the composition that they scarcely seem to communicate with each other. An iconographic novelty is the importance given to Joseph, who is emphasised by his red tunic.

Another work by Hans Memling in the Prado is the *Virgin and Child between two Angels* (Ref. No. 2543, ca. 1480).

THE REFORMATION AND EARLY 16TH CENTURY NORTHERN ART

HIERONYMUS BOSCH (ca. 1450–1516)
The Garden of Earthly Delights, ca. 1505
Triptych on panel, 220 x 195 cm.
REF. NO. 2823

Hieronymus van Aeken Bosch, known in Spain as El Bosco, was a contemporary of Leonardo da Vinci. He lived in the city of Hertogenbosch, commonly known as Den Bosch, from whence he derived his name. According to the limited amount of information that we have about him, he worked in complete isolation, studying astrology, astronomy and travel books with enormous interest. Despite this isolation, however, he had contacts with leading religious figures of the time. In his painting he developed a highly original and personal style and iconography.

The Garden of Earthly Delights is the most refined and complex of his paintings. It consists of a large triptych more than 2 metres high, whose overall theme is still difficult to specify: at the end of the 16th century it was described as a "painting of luxuriousness". One interpretation has associated the closed triptych with a representation of the world submerged by the waters. Open, the central panel would represent the world before the Great Flood, seen from a very high viewpoint, with a narrow strip of sky and men and women of different races depicted nude, forming various groups that carry out different acts. In the left panel are the Earthly Paradise and the Creation of Eve, and on the right is Hell with its horrible tortures, together with a satire of the Church, above all the Church's practice of selling indulgences. Together, the two symbolise the origins of Original Sin and its punishment.

Despite the importance of this painting, its function is not known, as it seems unlikely that it could have been an altarpiece.

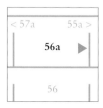

HIERONYMUS BOSCH (ca. 1450–1516)
The Haywain, ca. 1510
Triptych on panel, 135 x 190 cm.
REF. NO. 2052

The title of this painting is based on a Flemish proverb: "The world is like a haywain, and every man grabs what he can". It can also be related to a passage in Isaiah: "All flesh is grass and all glory like the flowers of the field". When closed, this triptych represents the path of life with a traveller and the perils of the journey. When open, it depicts the haywain in the centre symbolising the pleasures of the flesh, followed by the pope, the emperor, the king and other figures who attempt to climb onto it but are crushed to death. On the left wing is the Earthly Paradise with the creation of Eve, the Temptation and Expulsion from Paradise. On the right wing is Hell, the building of a tower and various tortures. The triptych is signed on the central panel in black letters: HIERONIMUS BOSCH.

No other work of this date could be further from the spirit of the Renaissance with regard to its content. Bosch emphasises the fragility and weakness of Man, in contrast to the exalted Renaissance image of him.

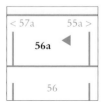

JOACHIM PATINIR (ca. 1480–1524)

Crossing the Styx, ca. 1515
Panel painting, 64 x 103 cm.
REF. NO. 1616

During his brief and little-documented career, Patinir devoted himself largely to painting "composite landscape", meaning landscapes with figures and a narrative element, specialising to an unparalleled degree in the genre of landscape for this period. The poet and art critic Yves Bonnefoy has pointed out the importance which landscape acquired from this time onwards, and noted that, interestingly, it was just as religion began to loose its all–powerful grip that man started to look for a realm which he could identify with.

The subject of the painting is derived more closely from Dante and from classical antiquity than from the Medieval Christian world. In Greek mythology, Charon steered his boat carrying the dead to Hades (the Underworld), crossing the Styx to reach Hell. In this case, Patinir has emphasised the broad landscape divided by the Styx: on one side is the Christian Paradise as indicated by the angel; on the other is Hell, with its entrance guarded by Cerberus and a fiery and desolate landscape in the background. However, the direction of the boat and Charon's expression indicate that he has decided to set out for that destination.

< 57a ▲   55a >

56a

56

FLEMISH SCHOOL. SECOND HALF

OF THE 16TH CENTURY

PIETER BRUEGEL "THE ELDER" (ca. 1525–1569)
The Triumph of Death, ca. 1560
Panel painting, 117 x 162 cm.
REF. NO. 1393

Pieter Bruegel "the Elder" was one of the earliest painters to specialise in landscape. Although he has sometimes been known as Peasant Bruegel, due to his numerous depictions of peasant life, he was not himself a peasant, but a highly cultivated man who had travelled in Italy where he sketched landscapes and city views. He began his artistic career making satirical prints along the line of Bosch, and it was only in 1650 that he began to paint landscapes for wealthy and intellectual Antwerp bankers.

The present work depicts the army of Death driving forward and scourging the human race — represented here by all classes of society — to its ultimate end. Death, on its dun–coloured horse, leads his skeleton army. On the way Bruegel depicts various scenes (in the left corner a skeleton shows a king that the sands of time in his hourglass have run out, while another rummages through his treasure), all treated with a mordant, satirical humour. The background includes mountains with glowing fires. As in paintings by Patinir, the high horizon line allows for the depiction of a panoramic landscape. The subject of Bruegel's painting is related to the Italian tradition of the Triumph of Death, but more closely to the northern pictorial type known as the "Dance of Death". The various different types of sin are differentiated, including avarice, luxuriousness and envy, while the moralising message is "death waits for no man".

< 57a   55a >

56a

56

ALBRECHT DÜRER (1471–1528)
Self-portrait, 1498
Oil on panel, 52 x 41 cm.
REF. NO. 2179

Within the context of International Humanism, Albrecht Dürer created an equivalent in the North of Europe to the Italian Quattrocento. Like many Florentine artists, he began his career in a goldsmith's studio — his father's — and then continued his studies with a painter in Nuremberg, where he also learned the art of engraving. Dürer considered that "art (*Kunst*) is in nature, and it is a question of extracting it... Art is learned and achieved by study, which takes seed, grows and flowers in this way". A proof of this approach are the hundreds of his drawings which have survived to today (over 1,600), and Dürer seems to have had an insatiable need to draw what he saw, including his own body and face. Few earlier artists have depicted themselves on so many occasions. At a time when it was rare for artists to sign their works, even important, finished ones, Dürer placed his initials (AD) even on preparatory drawings. He was also deeply concerned over his social status; in Italy at that time, artists were much more highly regarded and valued than in Germany and Dürer called this issue into question, painting himself in courtly dress.

The Prado self-portrait seems to be his first independent one. The format is half-length and shows the importance Dürer gave to the hands in his portraits. He is positioned seated near a window, through which we can see a landscape with snowy mountains in the background. On the window sill in white letters is an inscription in German: *1498 Das Malt Ich nach meiner Gestalt war sex und zwanzig Jor alt. Albrecht Dürer* (I painted this according to my appearance. I was twenty-six).

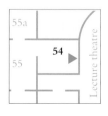

ALBRECHT DÜRER (1471–1528)

Adam and *Eve*, 1507
Panel painting, 209 x 81 cm. each
REF. NO. 2177 AND REF. NO. 2178

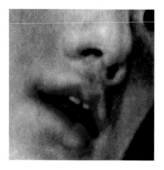

These two panels were a commission probably painted in Nuremberg after Dürer's return from his second Italian trip. Here his style reveals a synthesis of the Germanic and Italian approaches, with the biblical subject a mere pretext. What really interests Dürer here is the representation of the human body, and his study and investigation of this subject would result in a treatise on proportions and perspective that remained in use by northern artists for many years.

The Germanic element is evident in the cool colouring, the precise detail and the realistic approach with its expressionistic leanings, while the painstaking draughtsmanship is derived from Italy. In both cases Dürer focuses on the German and Italian canons of classical beauty with regard to the nude, and the subject matter of the panels is therefore ideal for this purpose. The bodies appear even more sculptural due to the use of black backgrounds.

Another interesting work by Dürer in the Prado is the *Portrait of an Unknown Man* (Ref. No. 2180, ca. 1521).

In the sixteenth century the portrait became an important genre due to the new emphasis on the personality of the individual as well as the practical function which these paintings fulfilled at the various European courts. In addition, to be depicted by an artist such as Anthonis Mor or Titian was a mark of prestige to which the highest court officials and nobles aspired. The court of Philip II in Spain as well as the Imperial courts of Rudolf II and Maximilian II were two centres where the genre was cultivated with great interest and originality, as we can see in the paintings of Alonso Sánchez Coello (see page 62), Anthonis Mor and Cristóbal de Morales.

ANTHONIS MOR — ANTONIO MORO, (ca. 1519–1576)
Mary Tudor, 1554
Panel painting, 109 x 84 cm.
REF. NO. 2108

Antonio Moro (or Anthonis Mor, as he is known in England) is considered the finest Flemish portrait painter working in the second half of the sixteenth century and the first artist whose innovations in the genre of portraiture would be taken up by Velázquez. Mor was court painter to Philip II, who ordered him to Spain from Flanders where the artist had already worked for Charles V. One of the works which he executed for the emperor was the portrait of Mary Tudor, the queen who briefly returned England to the Catholic faith, a key element in Charles V's efforts to arrange a marriage between Mary (queen of England since 1553) and his son Philip II. Mor was commissioned to produce this portrait of the potential bride in 1554, painting her with queenly dignity. In her hand Mary holds the Tudor rose, a dynastic symbol. She sits very upright on a red velvet throne wearing a wealth of jewels at her neck and on her wrists and fingers, emphasising her elevated rank, perhaps with the intention of impressing the Spanish court.

At the beginning of the sixteenth century, when the art of Giovanni Bellini still enjoyed great prestige, two young artists started to make their mark on Venetian art: Giorgione and Titian. The Prado's collection includes a fine group of paintings by these artists resulting from the interest of both Charles V and Philip II in their work. They are represented by portraits, mythological and religious paintings.

TITIAN — TIZIANO VECELLIO — (ca. 1490–1576)
Charles V at Mühlberg, 1548
Oil on canvas, 335 x 283 cm.
REF. NO. 410

In 1548, Titian was invited to present himself at Augsburg in order to paint a portrait of Charles V commemorating his recent victory at Mühlberg over the German Protestants. He was already extremely famous throughout Europe as a painter of portraits by this date, and the emperor was particularly appreciative of his work, having already commissioned a number of paintings. The iconography which Titian developed for this portrait was totally new, consisting of a full–length figure on horseback, derived from images of Roman emperors and possibly suggested by the emperor himself, although Titian had described such a format in a letter of 1547. The portrait, which is totally devoid of any symbolic element referring to Charles's victory, shows a solitary victor in the middle of the battle–field, wearing a cuirass and clutching a lance in readiness for combat. The emperor's expression, however, is not that of a warrior ready to attack, but rather of a figure meditating on victory, placed within a natural setting which heightens the supernatural character of the whole.

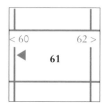

TITIAN — TIZIANO VECELLIO — (ca. 1490–1576)
Danaë and the Shower of Gold, 1554
Oil on canvas, 129 x 180 cm.
REF. NO. 425

This canvas is the first mythological painting that Titian executed for Philip II. It was completed in the summer of 1554 and was intended to decorate one of the king's private rooms in the Alcázar in Madrid. The paintings that make up this cycle, based on Book IV of Ovid's *Metamorphoses*, were described as "poesie". Ovid's text recounts how Acrisius, son of Abas and king of Argos, had been warned by an oracle that he would be overthrown by his grandson. For this reason he locked up his daughter Danaë in a tower. Jupiter, however, succeeded in thwarting Acrisius's efforts by transforming himself into a shower of gold.

In this canvas, in contrast to his earlier representations of the subject, Titian painted Danaë in a frontal pose, with the aim, according to a passage in a letter by the artist, of producing an effect of greater sensuality on the spectator. In addition, Titian introduces an iconographic novelty here: instead of the figure of Cupid, he depicts a servant, who moves forward to collect the shower of gold. Titian thus contrasts the cupidity and corruption of the nurse with the innocent, idealised character of the young girl, whose amorous encounter with Jupiter would result in the birth of Perseus.

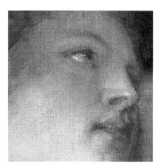

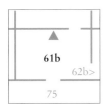

61b

62b>

75

PAOLO CALIARI, IL VERONESE (1528–1588)
The Infant Moses rescued from the River Nile, ca. 1580
Oil on canvas, 50 x 43 cm.
REF. NO. 502

Following Titian's death, the two leading painters in Venice were former pupils of the master: Tintoretto and Veronese. The latter, despite his name, deriving from his place of birth in Verona, is in some ways more Venetian than Titian, in the sense that more of his works were to be found there, due to the numerous commissions he carried out in the city. Veronese's paintings rely on an interplay of dramatic contrasts of light and colour, combining brilliant colours with areas in dark shadow. His work has influenced a wide variety of very different artists, from Giovanni Battista Tiepolo to Delacroix in the 19th century.

The subject of the present painting is derived from the Old Testament, and depicts the moment when Moses is rescued from the Nile by the Pharaoh's daughter who gave him an Egyptian name meaning "saved from the waters". Veronese gave the scene a contemporary setting and the characters wear 16th-century Venetian dress. From the 1570s his work was permeated by an arcadian vision of nature. The setting of the present painting, one of his finest, is a landscape with a city in the background, while the foreground trees seem to echo the rhythm of the figures. The drama of the scene is focussed on the presentation of the child rescued from the river: all eyes are turned to Pharaoh's daughter while she looks at the new-born child. The depiction of the water and of the child can be related to the ideas of birth and baptism, signifying salvation through water.

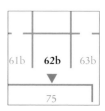

61b | **62b** | 63b

▼

75

691.

JACOPO ROBUSTI, IL TINTORETTO (1518–1594)
Christ washing the Disciples' Feet, ca. 1547
Oil on canvas, 210 x 533 cm.
REF. NO. 2824

Tintoretto began his career in Titian's studio where he made a close study of his technique, although later he developed his own particular style which involved pronounced, at times irrational, effects of perspective and foreshortening and gesticulating figures. All this contributed to the much–repeated cliché that he combined the colouring of Titian with the draughtsmanship of Michelangelo. An artist of great religious sensibility, he was much in demand as a painter of altarpieces in Venice and also painted numerous portraits. Tintoretto was also an extremely versatile artist, who was able to adapt himself to the commission in hand to the extent that he could change his style entirely to suit it, even to the point of imitating the work of other artists.

The present painting depicts the moment when Christ washes Saint Peter's feet. However, looking at the painting directly, this episode is relegated to a secondary level, while the important element is the architectural setting, which is inspired by the illustrations to Sebastiano Serlio's *Libro di perspettiva*. The contrasting colours bathed in a cool light introduce a new direction in Venetian painting, while the poses and gestures of the figures and the dog in the foreground give the work a markedly theatrical air.

The canvas was painted at a period when Tintoretto was experimenting with effects of perspective, and this aspect of the painting its essential to understanding its full meaning: if we place ourselves to the right and look at the composition from this angle, the picture space arranges itself along a diagonal starting with the episode of Christ washing Peter's feet, then moving on to the table with the Apostles and terminating in the triumphal arch at the end of the canal. The arch is the vanishing point of the painting, and viewed from the correct angle the empty spaces between the figures disappear. Above Christ's head, in an adjoining room, we can see through the archway a scene of the Last Supper.

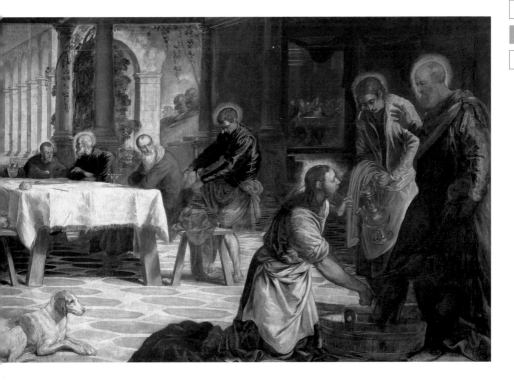

Domenikos Theotocopoulos, El Greco (1541–1614)
The Knight with his Hand on his Breast, ca. 1578
Oil on canvas, 81 x 66 cm.
Ref. no. 809

Domenikos Theotocopoulos was born in Crete, at that time under Venetian rule. He is documented in Venice at a young age, where he is known to have painted Byzantine–style icons for the Greek community. However, he was soon fascinated by the work of Titian, Tintoretto and later Michelangelo. He travelled to Rome, which was in the grip of the Counter–reformation; thus, any depiction of a religious subject was examined with fierce critical scrutiny. This was the time when Michelangelo's *Last Judgement* was condemned as heretical, and it seems that it was El Greco who offered to paint "something more decent and of better quality", an anecdote which gives some evidence of the extremely high opinion which the artist had of his own work. From 1567 El Greco lived in Spain, the ideal country at that time for someone of his spirituality. The destruction of the Turkish fleet at the Battle of Lepanto in 1571, the rise of the Counter–reformation, the appearance of the great mystical writers such as Saint Teresa and Saint John of the Cross, and the organisation of Spanish society, both with regard to the hierarchy of the Church and Court, made Spain the great bulwark of Christianity.

The present portrait has become the quintessential image of a Spanish nobleman at the time of Philip II. The sitter is depicted at the moment when he makes a promise and commits himself to its execution. The sword at his side is a sign of his noble rank. In contrast to his religious paintings, in his portraits El Greco was more inclined to accept the appearance of reality and not to alter the volumes of his figures. He was a consummate portraitist, delving profoundly into the characters of his sitters.

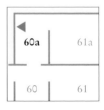

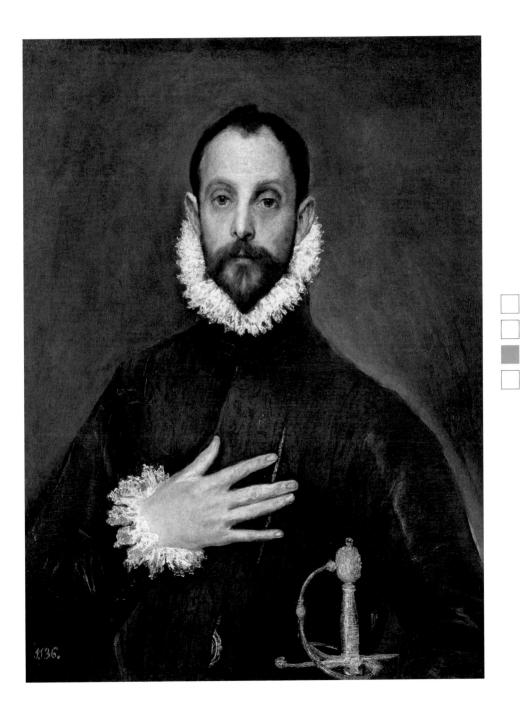

DOMENIKOS THEOTOCOPOULOS, EL GRECO (1541–1614)
The Resurrection, ca. 1597/1604
Oil on canvas, 275 x 127 cm.
REF. NO. 825

In this work painted towards the end of his career, El Greco uses a totally free style of brushstroke, while colour is deployed to heighten expressivity. Christ's two hands, each one arranged in a different position and direction, add movement to the upper part of the composition. The figures are lengthened to achieve the greatest sense of tension, while the arms of the figures on the lower level emphasise their expressions. The foreshortening of the figure who falls backwards at the sight of the Risen Christ contrasts with the image of the kneeling man in the helmet, who is half asleep and seems unaware of events. Both the treatment of the light and the arrangement of the figures in space go beyond the rational, revealing El Greco's most visionary side. He even changes the traditional mode of representing this subject, with the soldiers sleeping by the tomb, as El Greco omits the tomb, so that the subject seems to be half way between an Ascension and the Resurrection.

While Christ's banner symbolises His triumph over death, the purple cloak symbolises sacrifice and martyrdom.

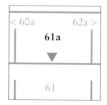

< 60a   62a >

61a

▼

61

ALONSO SÁNCHEZ COELLO (ca. 1532–1588)
The Infanta Isabel Clara Eugenia, 1579
Oil on canvas, 116 x 102 cm.
REF. NO. 1137

Mor's style formed the basis for the portraits of Philip II and his court, combined with elements derived from Titian. Portraits of this date depict figures imprisoned and tightly corseted in their clothes from which only their faces escape, occasionally endowed with an almost human expression.

The artist who best represents this style is Alonso Sánchez Coello. Born in the region of Valencia, he was painter to Philip II with whom he had a close relationship, to the extent that the king was godfather to one of the artist's children.

The present portrait depicts Isabel Clara Eugenia, daughter of Philip II and his third wife, Isabel de Valois. Born in Valsaín (Segovia) on 12 August 1566, in 1599 she married the Archduke of Austria and died in Brussels on 1 December 1633. This format of portrait left the artist with little compositional freedom. The sitter occupies the entire central part of the canvas from top to bottom. Standing and three–quarter length, she leans her arm on a chair. Sánchez Coello deployed a highly detailed and painstaking technique in his portraits, evident here in the jewels and the embroidery on the Infanta's dress.

The Prado's sculpture collection comprises around 220 works, most of them free-standing but also including a number of reliefs. Almost all of them were brought from Italy between the 16th and 19th centuries, giving the collection a certain coherence. There are some fragments of archaic Greek sculpture but a significant proportion of the collection consists of Roman sculpture which imitated and absorbed the lessons of classical Greek sculpture. In addition, that strand of Roman sculpture which gave rise to realistic portraits and sarcophagus decoration, and which would be the origin of paleo–Christian art, is also represented in the museum. Among later sculpture, the period spent by the Leoni (Leone Leoni and his son Pompeo) at the courts of Charles V and Philip II is well represented. Another important section is the so–called Room of the Muses which houses the sculpture collection of Queen Christina of Sweden, purchased after her death by Philip V and Isabella Farnese.

> *Bust of Antinous*, ca. 131 AD
> Fine–grained white marble, probably Carrara, height 97 cm.
> REF. NO. E–60

The figure represented, Antinous (ca. 110–130 AD), was a young slave from Bithynia in Asia Minor who entered Hadrian's entourage aged around thirteen and remained with the Emperor until his mysterious death: "The Emperor lost his favourite Antinous during a trip along the Nile, and cried like a woman", after which he was deified on Hadrian's command. For this reason, his image is to be found on coins as well as represented in sculpture. The traditional idealised, Greek classicism has been modified here by the side turn of the head and the downward gazes, giving the portrait a new sensibility, with a hint of melancholy.

(1) *Hypnos*, ca. 150 BC
     REF. NO. E–89

This sculpture is a personification of Sleep (*hypnos*), brother of Death, son of the Night and of Erebus (darkness and the Underworld). Hypnos flies around the world, making the living sleepy. This sculpture can be considered the best surviving version of the subject. It is a Roman copy of an original Greek sculpture which some critics have attributed to the School of Praxiteles, dating from the beginning of the third century BC, while others have described it as Neo–Attic of the mid–second century BC.

(2) *Sarcophagus with the Story of Achilles and Polyxena*, ca. 230 BC
     REF. NOS. E–118, E–120, E–180, E–182

This incomplete and fragmentary sarcophagus is of great interest as its iconography is unique. The story, which was appropriate due to its tragic nature, is narrated here in various episodes. On the long side we see the ceremony of armistice agreed between the Acheans and the Trojans to celebrate the wedding of Achilles and the Trojan princess Polyxena. We can easily make out Agamemnon in the centre between Ulysses and Paris, the latter with the head restored. The shorter side on the right shows the breaking of the truce, when Achilles falls dead having been wounded in the heel by Paris. The left end represents Polyxena going to her own sacrifice in honour of the dead hero, accompanied by various Acheans, among them Neoptolemus, son of Achilles. The other long side, now lost, but of which a piece survives in the Louvre, showed a combat between Acheans and Trojans.

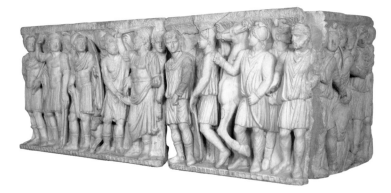

(2)

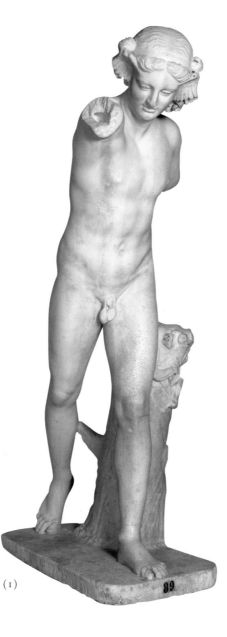

(1)

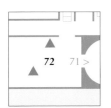

The San Ildefonso Group
Neo–Attic, Roman School, First century AD
Fine–grained white marble, height 161 cm.
REF. NO. E–28

The iconography of this group has been interpreted in variety of ways. The first and most likely reading is that the figures are the Dioscuri, the twins Castor and Pollux, sons of Zeus and Leda (wife of Tyndareus, king of Sparta). Castor was mortal, while Pollux was divine. The capture of the betrothed daughters of Leucippus resulted in a combat during which Castor died. Pollux then pleaded for his brother's immortality from Zeus. Here, both brothers are probably depicted making a thanks offering to the goddess of the Underworld, Persephone. In the 18th century Winckelmann suggested a different interpretation, that of Orestes and Pylades at the tomb of Agamemnon, offering a sacrifice to the statue of Artemesia, which they are attempting to appropriate.

The sculpture falls within the Neo–Attic tendency of late Hellenistic and Imperial sculpture. The figure with the torch is a softened variant of Polyclitus' style, while his companion imitates the pose of Praxiteles' *Apollo Sauroctonus* and the figure of the goddess is an attempt to imitate the Archaic style. With regard to a specific date, it should be placed between the end of the first century BC and the first half of the first century AD, representing the purified, classicising style found among Praxiteles' pupils in Naples.

The group belonged to the collection of Queen Christina of Sweden and was acquired in the early 18th century by Philip V and Isabella Farnese, who initially installed it at the palace of La Granja de San Ildefonso, hence its name. Visitors to La Granja can now see a cast of the sculpture on the pedestal which was designed for it.

First Floor

The term Baroque originally had a rather pejorative sense, implying "deviation from the norm". This is how 18th–century theoreticians regarded Baroque art, particularly the architecture, which seemed to them impure and irrational. Nonetheless, the 17th century, the century of Baroque art, was a complex one, in which other styles such as Realism and Classicism were also to be found. All shared a common spirit, albeit expressed through different styles. The history of 17th-century European art is peopled by major personalities such as Peter Paul Rubens, Nicolas Poussin, Gian Lorenzo Bernini, Anthony van Dyck, Diego Velázquez, Claude Lorraine and Rembrandt.

NICOLAS POUSSIN (1594–1665)
Mount Parnassus, ca. 1631–1632
Oil on canvas, 145 x 197 cm.
REF. NO. 2313

The two most important painters working in Rome in 1630 were both French: Nicolas Poussin and Claude Lorraine. Poussin arrived there in 1524 and soon gained the admiration of Roman intellectuals for his profound knowledge of classical literature. However, it proved harder for him to gain a leading place among the artists of the city. He worked for a while in Domenichino's workshop in the Palazzo Farnese, and in 1628 received an important commission for an altarpiece for Saint Peter's. This, however, was not well received, and from then on he decided not to accept any church or public commissions in Rome. He dedicated himself to easel paintings and to working for private clients who shared his intellectual interests.

The present painting is a celebration of the arts, particularly poetry. It depicts Apollo surrounded by the Nine Muses, from left to right: Thalia, Urania, Clio, Melpomene, Terpsichore, Erato, Polyhymnia, Euterpe and Calliope. Also surrounding Apollo are nine poets, and the god offers one of them a cup while Calliope crowns him with laurel. At their feet, a water nymph and two amorini are situated by a spring representing inspiration, clearly pointed out by the poet in the foreground on the right. The identity of the poets has long been a subject of speculation; the most likely interpretation is that of Panofsky who suggested that on the left are Homer and Virgil, while Tasso is in the right foreground. The poet who is being crowned is, according to Panofsky, a young poet called the cavaliere Marin who was Poussin's preferred poet and who had just died at a young age. It would seem that Poussin wished to identify himself as Raphael's successor as he was clearly inspired here by Raphael's painting *The Parnassus* on one of the walls in the Stanza della Segnatura in the Vatican, which he probably knew through the print by Marcantonio Raimondi.

CLAUDE LORRAINE (1600–1682)
Embarkation of Saint Paula Romana at Ostia, ca. 1630
Oil on canvas, 211 x 145 cm.
REF. NO. 2254

Claude Gellée, generally known as Claude Lorraine after the region of France where he was born, spent his adolescence in Rome where he learned to paint from a decorative painter of modest talent. Claude was the artist who invented the "Classical Landscape", whose compositional type and intellectualised approach would be widely taken up by later landscape painters around Europe, particularly English painters, and continued to be enormously influential many years later. Philip IV was extremely interested in this type of painting and the Prado therefore has an extensive representation of these landscapes. Claude's success was so great that around 1635 he decided to make a compilation of his autograph works in the form of drawings after them (later engraved). This book of drawings is now in the British Museum in London under the title of the *Liber Veritatis*.

Claude was inspired by the countryside around Rome, and he spent much time drawing outdoors, observing and noting every detail as well as the curving forms of the landscape under different types of light. His principal innovation was in the treatment of light, which seems to rise up from the horizon and spread out towards the spectator, reflected in the water, absorbed by the stone, filtering through the branches of the trees whose shadows are cast back into the interior of the picture space, creating a unified composition.

The present canvas depicts the port of Ostia with Saint Paula on the point of embarking for the Holy Land to join Saint Jerome. She is accompanied by her daughter Eustochium, who had also decided to devote herself to the religious life, while another of her daughters, Rufina, and her relations, implore her to remain with them. The scene depicted by Claude is therefore a dramatic one and a key moment in the life of the saint. The first rays of the sun appear over the horizon, piercing the cold and damp mist, while Saint Paula and her daughters descend the last steps to the quay where the boats are moored that will take them to the ship.

Other works by Claude Lorraine in the Prado include: the *Burial of Saint Serapia* (ca. 1637), and *Moses rescued from the Bullrushes* (ca. 1639), forming a pair; *The Archangel Raphael and Tobias* (ca. 1640), companion painting to the present one; *Landscape with Saint Onophrius* (ca. 1636); and *Landscape with the Temptations of Saint Anthony*.

GEORGES DE LA TOUR (1593–1652)
Blind Man playing the Hurdy–Gurdy, ca. 1640
Oil on canvas, 84 x 61 cm.
REF. NO. 7613

De la Tour was born in 1593 in Vic–sur–Seille, Lorraine. Of a humble family, his father was a baker. Between 1613 and 1616 he seems to have been absent from Lorraine and may have made a journey to Italy, as was normal in the training of young painters from Lorraine. He could therefore have acquired a direct knowledge of the work of Caravaggio that was to influence his later production.

De la Tour, however, is not a tenebrist painter in the manner of Caravaggio: he initially painted daylight scenes, while his night pieces have candles, thus differing from the almost complete darkness of Caravaggio's work. However, on a more profound level De la Tour was very close to the Italian artist's work in his search for a realism which was opposed to the Renaissance concept of forms, with the aim of conveying not a thought or a narrative, but rather the interior life of the figures captured in all their individuality. De la Tour soon absorbed this artistic revolution, and all the paintings from his early period profoundly reflect the spirit of Caravaggio even though they are daylight scenes, without lights, candles or torches. His "night" paintings would come later, when this vogue returned to favour.

It is impossible to understand the art of De la Tour without bearing in mind this paradoxical transition from one form of Caravaggism with its clear bright colours towards a visual nocturne which transcends any concept of reality. De la Tour knew how to balance the visual resources he had to hand at any stage of his career and with them to achieve the perfection of a work of art. The Prado's painting allows us a better appreciation of the handling of the paint. The artist used the tip of the brush, in an extremely precise manner, with a great variety of paint strokes and different effects, particularly noticeable in the hair. The artist's knowledge of colour is remarkable here, as is his highly refined use of a palette of colours of warm tones from beiges and ochres, to the hint of salmon pink on the belt.

The contrasts are pronounced, with the figure strongly highlighted in full light against the black background on the left, while the right part of the background is strongly lit. The effect of light coming from the left is particularly strong. The effect is to give a restrained authority to the volumes illuminated by harsh lighting from the side. The solidity of these volumes, the refinement and force of execution allow us to date this painting to late in the artist's career, around 1640. It may be the last daytime painting by De la Tour to have survived.

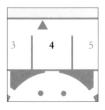

GUIDO RENI (1575–1642)
Atalanta and Hippomenes, ca. 1630
Oil on canvas, 206 x 297 cm.
REF. NO. 3090

Guido Reni was born in Bologna and lived in Rome. In his painting he adopted Caravaggio's dramatic use of chiaroscuro to increase the focus of attention on his figures. At the outset, his style is closely linked to Rubens, and his first teacher was in fact a Mannerist painter from Antwerp. However, he soon began to work within the classicising circles of the Carracci in Bologna.

The present painting falls within this style. The figures are like ballet dancers. Their gestures and poses have more to do with stylisation or mannerism that with any real function. The narrative derives from Ovid's *Metamorphoses*: Atalanta, a remarkably beautiful young woman, was also faster than any man at the race. She decreed that any successful suitor would have to beat her, but that any man who lost would die. This was the case until the arrival of Hippomenes, who beat her with the help of Venus. The goddess had given him three golden apples that he threw down during the race, thus delaying Atalanta who paused to pick them up. Reni depicts the moment when she stoops to pick up the third apple. The young bodies are painted as exceptionally soft, but with natural proportions and a sensuality in the flesh tones which is clearly indebted to Correggio. The composition is constructed like a low–relief, or perhaps like one of the ceiling paintings in the Palazzo Farnese, with the movement organised in parallel to the picture space.

17th Century Dutch and Flemish Painting

Rembrandt Harmensz van Rijn (1606–1669)
Artemisia, 1634
Oil on canvas, 142 x 153 cm.
Ref. no. 2132

Rembrandt Harmensz. van Rijn was a Dutch painter who spent his entire career in his native country, first in Leyden then in Amsterdam, where he lived from 1631.

His early works are biblical scenes whose spiral compositions are indebted to Rubens, enhanced by a strong chiaroscuro derived from Caravaggio's Dutch followers. One could describe all his work as a response to that of other artists, both European and non–European. All these influences were perfectly assimilated and absorbed in his work, which can be seen as an uninterrupted process of artistic and spiritual development. Between 1631 and 1632 he moved from Leyden to the prosperous city of Amsterdam, the economic centre of the Dutch Republic, where he soon established a reputation, particularly as a portrait painter. Rembrandt was one of the artists who most often painted himself, in some cases in the guise of a biblical or legendary character. Including studies, prints and oil paintings we have a total of more than 100 self–portraits, constituting nothing less than a visual autobiography. Among these, we should single out the self–portrait of 1656, painted at a difficult and unhappy time following his bankruptcy. Rembrandt here shows himself with white hair and a tired and troubled air. Baudelaire described him as the "lighthouse" of painting, and there is no doubt that Rembrandt should be considered among the greatest figures of European art.

The present painting depicts Artemisia, queen of Pergamon, seated by a table with a book on it and receiving the ashes of her husband in a chalice. To the left, a servant presents her with them, and we can make out an old woman in the background. It seems likely that the model for Artemisia is Rembrandt's wife Saskia, painted around the time of their marriage in a composition whose iconography refers to marital fidelity. An alternative subject is that of Sophonisba receiving the cup of poison sent by her husband Masinissa who is a prisoner: with it she can take her own life in order not to fall into the hands of Scipio.

The painting is, however, devoid of the drama that we would expect in such a subject. Rembrandt expresses an almost sublime impartiality and lack of emotion. The deep–seated belief that the human soul restricts itself to contemplation rather than to the sensual activation of the body may be related to the teachings of Arnold Geulincx, a pupil of Descartes in Leyden. The heavy figure of Artemisia reveals the workings of her inner thoughts, conveyed through a static pose and with the dignity of natural nobility.

PETER PAUL RUBENS (1577–1640)
The Three Graces, ca. 1635
Panel painting, 221 x 181 cm.
REF. NO. 1670

Peter Paul Rubens was born in Siegen (Westphalia) as his father, a renowned lawyer, was obliged to flee from Antwerp due to his Protestant faith. On the death of his father, Rubens returned to Antwerp where he converted to Catholicism, becoming a devout, stoical Catholic. He was educated to a high level before opting for painting as a career. He then trained with the history painter Otto van Veen, who first aroused his interest for Italy, where Rubens worked from 1600 to 1608 in the service of the court at Mantua. The Prado has two works from this date: *The Duke of Lerma* (ca. 1603) and *Saint George and the Dragon* (ca. 1606). On his return to Antwerp in 1609, where he was now highly regarded, he received important commissions for works such as the *Adoration of the Magi* (1609), also now in the Prado.

The Three Graces represents the daughters of Zeus and Eurynome who were virgins in the service of Venus and who aroused the sensation of the joy of life. The subject derives from classical mythology and was much depicted in art, particularly in sculpture. In his *Theogony* Hesiod names and describes them: Aglaia ("resplandescent"), Euphrosyne ("joyous"), Thalia ("flowering"). Rubens emphasises their role as companions of Venus, goddess of love, representing a cupid on top of the fountain at the upper right, and above their heads a garland of roses, Venus' flower. The artist conveys nothing less than a total life philosophy, an exaltation of the pleasures of the senses, also referring to his own life, as the three goddesses are portraits of his two wives, Isabelle Brandt and Hélène Fourment, alluding to the fact that it is they who have given him happiness, filling his life with beauty and pleasure. Rubens kept this painting throughout his life, having particular affection for it and considering it a sort of talisman.

The composition is completely classical: the figures are arranged in complimentary

poses, creating the impression of dynamic movement. Deciding against the fixed nature of a pyramidal composition, Rubens organised his composition as a sort of infinite space of intersections between one diagonal and another.

ANTHONY VAN DYCK (1599–1641)
Sir Endymion Porter and Van Dyck, ca. 1635
Oil on oval canvas, 115 x 141 cm.
REF. NO. 1489

Of the numerous assistants working in Rubens' studio, the most talented was Anthony van Dyck. He painted mythological and religious paintings, but was above all a famed portrait painter. The type of portrait he developed in England, while working at the court of Charles I, would remain in use for nearly two hundred years.

Van Dyck was born in Antwerp in 1599, seventh son of a prosperous merchant. His paternal grandfather was a painter, and there were also artists among his mother's family. In Antwerp, painting was a flourishing art form as well as a commercially lucrative one due to the numerous commissions from churches throughout the region. For this reason, it is not surprising that despite being from a wealthy family, Van Dyck was apprenticed to a painter at the age of ten. He was soon moving in the circle of Rubens and that artist's influence is evident in Van Dyck's first major altarpieces. The Prado has a fine selection of works from this period, including *The Taking of Christ*, *The Crowning with Thorns*, and *The Brazen Serpent*. His fame soon spread abroad and he was called to London (1620–1621), where he worked for the Duke of Buckingham and for James I. During this period, Van Dyck discovered the work of the Venetian painters, particularly Titian, from whom he learned his treatment of colour and play of light and shade, resulting in the need for a trip to Italy. In 1621 he travelled there, staying in Genoa, Rome and Palermo, returning to Antwerp in 1629. It was at that point that he painted the portrait of his friend Martin Ryckaert (ca. 1587–1631), also in the Prado.

In 1632 Van Dyck returned to London. Two years earlier, Sir Endymion Porter had purchased the artist's painting *Rinaldo and Armida* for Charles I of England. Charles prized Titian's work above all others, and the Titianesque style of Van Dyck's canvas led the king to see him as the Italian artist's successor.

The present canvas is the only one in which Van Dyck paints himself with another figure. Endymion Porter (1587–1649) was a travelled and cultured man, and a friend of the Duke of Buckingham, through whom he met Van Dyck around 1620. Van Dyck's pose is slightly unnatural and must have been awkward for him, but can be explained if we note that he has placed himself on a lower level, for reasons of protocol.

Van Dyck did not, however, move definitively to London until 1639. It was at this point that he married Mary Ruthven, lady–in–waiting to the Queen of England. The Prado has a wonderful, freely painted portrait of her by her husband.

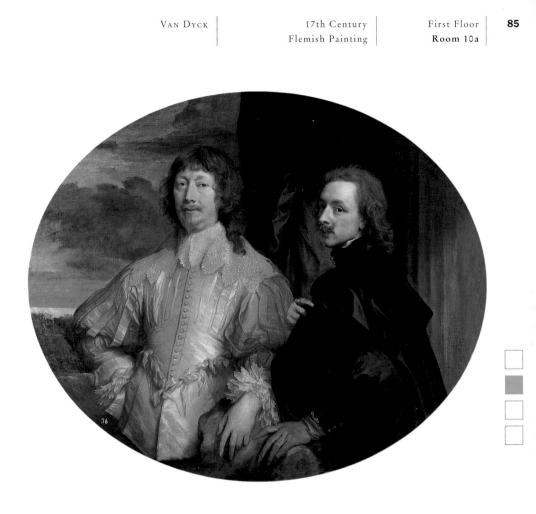

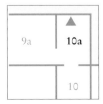

FRANCISCO DE RIBALTA (1565–1628)
Christ embracing Saint Bernard, ca. 1625
Oil on canvas, 158 x 113 cm.
REF. NO. 2804

Born in Solsona (Lleida), Francisco de Ribalta was trained in Madrid in the style of the artists working at El Escorial, but he spent most of his career in Valencia from 1599 until his death. He soon departed from the Mannerist style of the El Escorial artists, moving towards a type of naturalism that was to prove a high point of 17th–century Spanish Baroque painting.

This canvas was executed for the Carthusian monastery at Portacoeli (Valencia). It depicts a passage from the life of Saint Bernard, recounted for the first time in the 16th century in the text *Flos Sanctorum* (1599) by the monk Rivadeneyra, who recounts how the founder of the Cistercian order had a mystical vision in which Christ freed himself from the nails of the cross in order to bend down and embrace the saint. The subject is rarely depicted in art.

In the shadows behind we can make out two angels. The composition is realised from a low viewpoint, which gives it an obvious sense of monumentality. Christ takes His arms from the cross to enfold Saint Bernard in an embrace, while the saint seems to be suspended in a sensation of total confidence and faith. The light is Caravaggesque in the sense that it seems to come from a direction that lacks a natural source of light, entering from the left side and seeming to brush over the figures, fusing them into one element and giving them an almost tangible sense of sculptural volume.

24   25

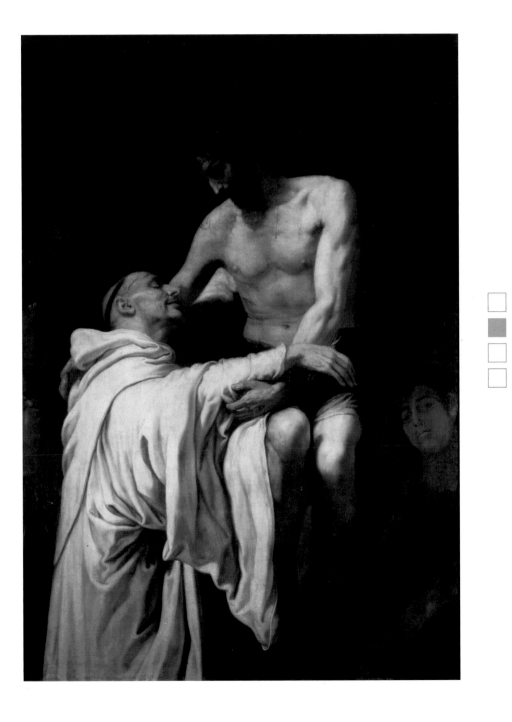

JOSÉ DE RIBERA, EL ESPAÑOLETO (1591–1652)
The Magdalen or Saint Thais, 1641
Oil on canvas, 182 x 149 cm.
REF. NO. 1103

José de Ribera was born in Játiva (Valencia) into a humble family. He soon moved to Valencia where he may have met the leading Valencian artist of that time, Francisco de Ribalta. Ribera lived in Naples from 1616 until the end of his life, gaining the nickname of "El Españoleto". For the Romantics, he was the prototype of the anti-classical and of the Spanish, particularly for his representation of martyrdoms "in all their brutality". Lord Byron, for example, wrote that Ribera "wet his brushes in the blood of the saints". This Romantic and exaggerated image of Spain spread throughout Europe due to a widespread ignorance of the country. Nonetheless, Ribera painted some of the most beautiful images of women in the whole of Spanish art.

The present painting is one of a group of four hermit saints depicted against a remote, extensive and light–filled landscape setting. All these paintings are now in the Prado. Two represent young saints, the present one and *Saint John the Baptist*, while *Saint Mary the Egyptian* and *Saint Bartholomew* are depicted as very old, worn away by penitence and fasting, but still imbued with a delicate nobility. Their bodies seem to be illuminated in an almost supernatural way, placed in a darkened setting (in the case of the Magdalen, against some sombre rocks) in a manner which again seems to be derived from Caravaggio as it is difficult to identify the light source.

The features of the Magdalen seem to be those of the painter's daughter. Mary Magdalen, a woman of loose morals identified in the Bible as Mary of Magdala, became the model of devout conversion. According to legend, she retired to the desert as a penitent. Ribera's knowledge of the nude as revealed here must have been gained through Italian art. In the late 1640s illness obliged him to interrupt some of his most important commissions. This had been his most successful decade in which he had received a very large number of commissions, built a palatial house in Naples and earned large sums of money. His work of this period is luminous and transparent.

24

25

Velázquez was born in Seville in 1599. He trained with the painter Francisco Pacheco (1564–1654), a highly cultured artist. The Academy which Pacheco founded was dominated by a Christian Neo–platonism, following the Jesuit rule of representing the invisible through the accurate evocation of the senses and using the experiences of everyday reality to convey a concept. These precepts were enriched by the new aesthetic developed by Caravaggio. In 1621 Philip IV came to the throne. Of rather apathetic character, he left the government of the country in the hands of the Count Duke of Olivares, who was of Andalucian origin. The route to Court for Andalucians was therefore facilitated, as in the case of Velázquez, through the influence of Pacheco. During his second trip to Madrid Velázquez painted the *Portrait of Philip IV* (in the Prado, Ref. No. 1182) and was named Court Painter. The years between 1623 and 1629 (he left for Italy in the latter year) were mainly devoted to portraiture. Velázquez's work represents a complete revival of the great pictorial genres: portraiture, landscape, historical and mythological painting.

DIEGO VELÁZQUEZ (1599–1660)
Los Borrachos or *The Triumph of Bacchus*, ca. 1625
Oil on canvas, 165 x 225 cm.
REF. NO. 1170

Velázquez invents a new way of seeing the mythological story of Bacchus. The semi–naked figure of Bacchus, accompanied by a satyr, is surrounded by the sort of humble and rather low–life drinkers who would have been found in any Madrid street, inn or tavern.

The painting divides into two parts, with the left hand part dedicated to the young god and the satyr who are depicted with the sexual ambiguity found in Caravaggio's representation of such young males. The right hand side of the painting features the popular types who kneel before the god while one of them makes contact with the spectator by looking straight out and raising his glass in a toast. This is a remarkably silent and motionless bacchanal. The carefully organised composition, with the figures arranged in a sort of cross formation, is placed in front of a Castillian landscape. Velázquez has created a pictorial discourse on the blessings of wine and its powers to console men in the face of the troubles of daily life.

With regard to his treatment of a Bacchic subject, Velázquez here makes a statement of his independence and artistic self–confidence, expressing his own artistic ideology.

The painting is also a mythological triumph represented in the particular style of the artist, in which qualities such as gravity and irony, severity and cynicism are juxtaposed and complement each other, as we can see from the expression of the young god.

DIEGO VELÁZQUEZ (1599–1660)
Las Meninas, or *The Family of Philip IV*, ca. 1656
Oil on canvas, 318 x 276 cm.
REF. NO. 1174

No–one could dispute that, with regard to the quality of its execution, this is the most perfect painting in the history of 17th–century European painting. The subject of the painting has been interpreted in numerous ways. For many, it is an example of how realistic subjects can have hidden behind them a highly complex world of meanings. The episode depicted takes place in the Alcázar in Madrid, in a room that was reserved for the use of court painters. What we actually see is the arrival in Velázquez' studio of the Infanta Margarita, daughter of Philip IV and his second wife Mariana of Austria, whose portrait the artist may actually be painting at this point, possibly in the presence of the royal couple. Most of the figures look out towards the spectator who is placed in front of the scene, in the spot where the monarchs might be expected to be, while the centre of the composition is occupied by the Infanta Margarita. To each side of her are her maids or "meninas", doña María Agustina Sarmiento, who offers her a tray with a little jug of water, and doña Isabel Velasco. Next to her are the dwarves Maribárbola and Nicolás de Pertusato. In the middle ground are doña Marcela de Ulloa, guardian of the queen's ladies, and next to her a lightly–sketched man dressed in black with his hands at his belt, presumably another court servant who looked after the queen's maids.

Velázquez paints himself to the left of the painting, pausing to reflect on the painting which he is executing. The monarchs are reflected in the mirror on the end wall in the background. Next to the mirror is a half–open door and standing in it looking at the scene is José Nieto, also a court Chamberlain. Hanging on the back wall are paintings by Rubens' studio. Velázquez wears at his waist the key that indicates his rank as Palace Chamberlain, as well as the noble cross of Santiago on his breast. The presence of an artist with these social attributes, depicted as reflecting on art itself in the presence of the monarchs and other members of the royal family, is a clear affirmation on Velázquez's part of the nobility of the art of painting.

The perspectival construction of this composition is a complex, mathematical one, and a subtle meditation on representation itself, on the laws which govern sight and on the relationship between the painted surface, a suggested space, and the psychological space inhabited by the spectator. The painting also allows for a political reading regarding Philip's hopes for the succession, which at that time rested on the Infanta Margarita. Above all else, *Las Meninas* is a demonstration of the painter's power to represent life, which acquires a real presence before our eyes and for one moment succeeds in stopping time itself.

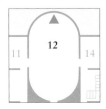

Diego Velázquez (1599–1660)
The Spinners, or *The Fable of Arachne*, 1657
Oil on canvas, 220 x 289 cm.
Ref. no. 1173

The most realistic and least symbolic interpretations of this painting have seen it as the visit of three ladies (one of them possibly from the Royal Family) to the Santa Isabel Tapestry Manufactory. However, behind the everyday event lies a representation of the bet between Pallas Athena (Minerva) and Arachne, a young woman from Lydia: "Arachne was greatly famed throughout the cities of Lydia, although born into a humble family...and it was not just a joy to see her finished clothes, but also how she made them... it was obvious that she was a pupil of Athena. But she denied it, which offended her great teacher who said, Let her compete with me!..." (Ovid, *Metamorphoses*, Book VI). The story centres on the ideas of pride and of a mortal competing with a goddess, aggravated by Arachne's lack of tact in depicting on one of the tapestries in the competition the foibles of Jupiter (father of Minerva), among them the Rape of Europa. This can be seen in the tapestry in the background, reproducing Titian's painting of the subject, along with the three courtly ladies, Pallas Athena in armour and Arachne, all in front of the tapestry. Athena punishes the young girl for her presumption, turning her into a spider. The antidote to her poison is music, hence the presence of the instrument in the painting. The weavers in the foreground might again be Pallas Athena and Arachne. The light falls directly onto the back of the young woman (Arachne) who is unwinding the thread onto a frame, while the old woman on the left (Athena) makes her wheel spin so fast that its spokes disappear; their movement is conveyed by the blurred radii of the spokes, an extraordinary representation of speed centuries before Futurism and photography. The poses of these two women are based on Michelangelo's nudes on the ceiling of the Sistine Chapel, another example of Velázquez's touches of humour.

The present painting could be described as the construction of a "painting within a painting", while the whole scene has been interpreted as an allegory of the nobility of painting. It could be read as a description of the creative process, which includes a manual phase and a purely intellectual phase that has an almost divine nature and requires that the creator be illuminated by the light of an idea that has to be "judged" and evaluated. The original format of the painting was considerably smaller; 50 cm were added later to the upper part and 37 cm to the sides, considerably altering Velázquez's original composition.

DIEGO VELÁZQUEZ (1599–1660)
The Lances, or *The Surrender of Breda*, 1634–1635
Oil on canvas, 307 x 367 cm.
REF. NO. 1172

This was one of the paintings of historical subjects that decorated the Salón de Reinos in the Buen Retiro Palace in Madrid. The surrender of Breda took place on 2 June 1625, while the handing over the keys of the city was made three days later. They were among the episodes that took place during the revolt of the Low Countries which would finally result in their independence from Spain in 1639. This victory was the subject of a significant propaganda campaign, among which featured Jacques Callot's prints and the paintings of Peeter Snayers. Velázquez, however, avoided this panegyric vision of victory. Against the background of a landscape with still burning fires of war and destruction, the artist depicts the moment when Ambrogio Spinola, the Genoese general in command of the Flemish troops, receives from the Dutch governor, Justin of Nassau, the keys of the city of Breda. Velázquez seems to have been inspired by a scene in the play *The Siege of Breda* by Pedro Calderón: "Justin, I receive [the keys] from you/ and know how valiant/ you are, and that the valour of the conquered/makes the conqueror famous".

In a brilliantly–constructed composition, the infantry regiments appear behind the two leaders, with their lances protruding from above their heads, creating a sort of grille which leads the eye back into the landscape in an astonishing effect of trompe l'oeil, also emphasising the discipline of the troops. The artist, however, arranges four of the lances at a sloping angle, adding to the realism and also emphasising the sloping line created by the flag and the general emphasis on oblique lines in the cross-shaped structure of the composition. Behind the figure of Justin are the Dutch who are fewer in number and more scattered, with shorter and less organised lances and halberds and stronger contrasts in the light and in their poses. Velázquez created the sensation of an outdoor scene in his studio on the basis of sketches. The landscape would have been taken from contemporary engravings, as he had not seen it at first hand.

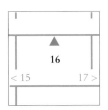

BARTOLOMÉ ESTEBAN MURILLO (1618–1682)
The Holy Family with the Bird, 1650
Oil on canvas, 144 x 188 cm.
REF. NO. 960

Among Spanish artists, Bartolomé Esteban Murillo was one of the most famous outside his native country, both during his own lifetime and later, in the 18th and 19th centuries. The Prado has a very large selection of his work, representative of every phase of his career. His early style showed the influence of Zurbarán's and Velázquez's realism, while his brushwork later becomes softer and his colouring more expressive and vibrant under the influence of Flemish and Venetian painting. The gentle piety of his religious compositions, which occasionally tend towards the sentimental, brought him enormous success. The present work was painted at a time when Murillo's style still showed a certain Caravaggesque realism filtered through Zurbarán's interpretation of that artist, using light to model the figures and objects, defining the atmosphere.

The Infant Christ holds a bird in His hand and leans against the seated Saint Joseph who point out the dog with one hand while he supports the Child with the other. On the left, the Virgin is winding a ball of thread with her sewing basket at her side. On the right is Saint Joseph's carpenter's bench.

Other works by Murillo in the Prado include: *The Adoration of the Magi* (ca. 1660); *The Good Shepherd* (ca. 1665); a pair of lunettes entitled *The Founding of Santa Maria Maggiore in Rome I: the dream of the Patriarch* (ca. 1665), and *The Founding of Santa Maria Maggiore in Rome II: the Patriarch reveals his Dream to the Pope* (ca. 1665).

< 27 **28** 29 >

FRANCISCO DE ZURBARÁN (1598–1664)
Still Life, 1602
Oil on canvas, 46 x 84 cm.
REF. NO. 2803

Francisco de Zurbarán (who was born in Fuente de Cantos, Badajoz, and died in Madrid) was trained as a painter in Seville. At an early stage he adopted a very individualised version of Caravaggio's style with sculptural volumes lit by strong contrasts of light and shade. His avoidance of unnecessary detail led to the creation of a static, silent pictorial universe. In 1634 he was in Madrid for a short period, probably invited by Velázquez to work on the decoration of the Buen Retiro. He returned to Seville and at that pointed painted his great cycles of paintings for various monasteries. He travelled to Madrid again in 1658 towards the end of his life at a time when he had few commissions from clients, and lived there until his death in very straightened

financial circumstances. The Prado has two important works from his early career: *The Apparition of Saint Peter to Saint Pedro Nolasco* (1626), and *The Vision of the Heavenly Jerusalem*. Slightly later is the *Immaculate Conception* (1630), an iconography very frequently depicted by the artist who would create an archetypal image of the Immaculate Virgin.

Zurbarán's still lifes are key works in Spanish 17th–century painting. The present painting is exceptionally realistic; notable are the extreme simplicity in the arrangement of the objects and the interest in placing the most everyday objects under an abstract light, bringing to mind the concept of a "poetic of painting". On a simple wooden table the artist arranges a row of four vessels made of different materials. With a dazzling simplicity, he recreates their different textures, mainly through his profound knowledge of the effects of light, through which he gives the vessels volume and a sense of real presence. According to the Italian art historian Longhi, their almost ritualistic arrangement evokes the placing of liturgical objects on the altar.

JUAN SÁNCHEZ COTÁN (ca. 1560–1627)
Still Life with Game, Vegetables and Fruit, 1602
Oil on canvas, 68 x 89 cm.
REF. NO. 7612

Juan Sánchez Cotán was one of the great masters of still life painting. He trained with the painter Blas de Prado, an artist who painted religious works and also fruit and flower pictures, which seem to have been highly appreciated but have not survived. Sánchez Cotán's still lifes are extremely original, very austere and sober in their presentation of the objects represented, creating an intensity of mood and atmosphere.

Leaning on the right–hand side of the ledge is a large pinkish–white cardoon. Next to it are two white radishes and three carrots, while the composition is closed on the left by six plucked small birds. Above are suspended three lemons, seven red apples hanging from strings and in the centre a pair of partridges and two smaller birds.

LUIS EGIDIO MELÉNDEZ (1716–1780)
Still Life with a Box of Sweetmeats, Round Loaf and other Objects, 1770
Oil on canvas, 49 x 37 cm.
REF. NO. 906

The 18th century saw a change in the content of still life paintings due to the influence of the Enlightenment and its impulse towards objective observation; an impulse which propelled Linnaeus to classify every known plant and animal according to its genus and species. In the second third of the century this trend became evident in still–life painting, which no longer symbolised the transience of life, but took on an independent value of its own. Thus it acquired meaning from the objects within it and their interrelationships. Meléndez developed a highly thought–out type of composition, painted with exquisite care in the representation of the elements within it. These objects are arranged not so much in the air but rather in a void, in the sense of isolating them from any sensation which might disturb the spectator's attention. This is fundamentally a material reality. The table is the base of the painting, forming the horizon against which the objects are arranged.

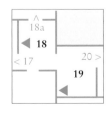

Sánchez Cotán
Meléndez

17th Century
Spanish Painting

First Floor
Rooms 18 and 19

103

Goya is among the artists best represented in the Prado. He lived and worked at the same time as the French painter Jacques–Louis David (1748–1825) who represents the spirit of classicism in painting. In comparison with the ideas of patriotism and honour expressed by David, Goya seems to us an artist whose work goes beyond his own age. He was painter to the Spanish Court but was also friend to many of the Spaniards who encouraged the ideas of the Enlightenment, sharing their hatred of injustice, fanaticism, religiosity and superstition. His aversion to cruelty led him to produce his first great series of prints, *Los Caprichos* (Caprices), published in 1799, the year he was made First Painter to the King. The inscriptions printed below the images reveal a desire to improve morality and behaviour. However, his portrait of a disconnected world inhabited by ignoble, barely human creatures with bestial appetites and inclinations reveals how far Goya had departed from the optimistic faith in the power of reason and the possibility of human progress upheld by the Enlightenment. These doubts strengthened to emotions of incredulity and desperation in the shocking series of prints entitled *Desastres de la Guerra* (Disasters of War), inspired by the atrocities committed by the French troops during the Peninsular War. Goya depicts this conflict (which gave rise to the first modern use of the word *guerilla*) through images of cruelty which go beyond moral protest, stripping away any vestige of nobility from the bodies and souls of both the victims and the victorious.

FRANCISCO DE GOYA (1746–1828)
Self–portrait, 1815
Oil on canvas, 46 x 35 cm.
REF. NO. 723

Goya painted a large number of self–portraits throughout his life, using various techniques. The present portrait is, along with the one now in the Academia de San Fernando, the most deeply–felt and sincere. The artist presents himself simply and directly without any reference to his status, profession, tastes or his important patrons. The date is thought to be around 1815 due to its relationship with the self–portrait in the Academia which is signed and dated to that year. The Prado painting may at first glance appear to be a copy of that one, but it is in fact a different version. There are differences in the position of the head and the way of painting the neck of the shirt. In addition the expression on the face varies between the two works: in the Academia version the expression is not so lively.

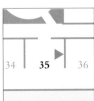

FRANCISCO DE GOYA (1746–1828)
The Family of Charles IV, 1800
Oil on canvas, 280 x 336 cm.
REF. NO. 726

In 1800 Charles IV expressed the wish to have a portrait of his entire family, and Goya travelled to Aranjuez to make studies of the family members who would be included in the work. Arranged in a frieze–like manner from left to right are: Carlos María Isidro; Goya himself painting; Ferdinand, Prince of Asturias; María Josefa, sister of Charles IV; an unknown princess with her face turned away who might be the future Princess of Asturias, who had not yet been chosen, or possibly another daughter of Charles IV, Carlota Joaquina, Queen of Portugal, who was not in Madrid at that time; María Isabel; Queen María Luisa; Francisco de Paula; King Charles IV who, like the Prince of Asturias, is placed further forward in the picture plane that the other figures; Antonio Pascual, the king's brother; and the princes of Parma, Luis de Borbón and his wife María Luisa Josefina, with their son Carlos Luis in her arms. Behind the Prince of Parma is another unknown woman, who again might be Carlota or María Amalia, another daughter of Charles IV who had died two years earlier. In the background is a wall hung with two paintings. Apart from Goya, all the men wear the sash of the Order of Charles III and some have the Order of the Golden Fleece. The king wears the insignias of the military orders and of the Portuguese Order of Christ. The women are dressed in the Empire style and wear the sash of the Order of María Luisa. The queen occupies the centre of the canvas and while the other family members are placed within a slightly receding area, as if standing at the back of a large salon. Goya succeeded in representing a closed world with little room to breathe. This portrait represents the culmination of Goya's official career. One year earlier he had been appointed Painter to the King.

The inclusion of Goya himself in the composition, rather hidden in the shadows on the far left in front of his easel, is a clear reference to the self portrait of Velázquez (whom he considered his master) in *Las Meninas*. However, Goya does not paint himself in the professional attitude which Velázquez adopted, but rather looks thoughtfully at the spectator. Although the royal family is represented in a room in a palace, Goya has avoided the use of complex perspectival structures. The wall directly behind the figures prevents any illusion of depth. Nor is a sense of depth encouraged by the monotonous arrangement of the figures in almost serried ranks as in a relief. Nonetheless, the play of light and shadow, the contrast of the sparkling highlights and the colour arranged in patches across the canvas, give variety to the composition and help to differentiate between the succession of the different planes into depth.

FRANCISCO DE GOYA (1746–1828)
The Third of May 1808 in Madrid: the Executions at Príncipe Pío, 1814
Oil on canvas, 268 x 347 cm.
REF. NO. 749

On 24 February 1814, Goya wrote to the Regent, Cardinal Luis de Borbón, not only to alert him to his financial difficulties, but also to offer to: "immortalise through painting the most notable and heroic actions and scenes of our glorious uprising against the tyrant of Europe". The Regent granted Goya 1,500 reales and the materials for producing two paintings. These were the present work, and the painting entitled *The Second of May 1808 in Madrid: the Charge of the Mameluks,* however, the intended destination of these paintings is unknown.

The painting dedicated to a "historical event", developed by Antoine Jean Gros in his *Napoleon and the Plague Victims at Jaffa* (1804), was a new type in which the emphasis is placed on realism rather than the idealism upheld by David, and became the model for Gros' generation, being widely known through engravings. According to the art historian Hugh Honour, Goya conceived his two paintings on the events of the second and third of May as following this "historical event" model. To the right, the ranks of soldiers prepare to fire: to the left a monk and five humble citizens face execution; on the ground are three corpses, and in the background a group of men sentenced to die. In the darkness of the background we can make out the skyline of Madrid. The focus of the drama falls on the man in the white shirt, kneeling with his arms outstretched in a cross in front of the faceless block of the firing squad.

Goya's canvas, painted just before the restoration of the Bourbon monarchy in 1814, was painted for public exhibition, as a commemoration of the start of the Spanish War of Independence (the Peninsular War) and was evidently meant to imply that the men who died in 1808 did not sacrifice themselves in vain. However, its meaning is deeper and broader than that, and there is no hope in this secular martyrdom that the evil of this world will be judged in the next. Rather, we see the humble working man sacrificed for pointless reasons.

Goya did not depict any particular national hero or general, and the protagonists of the painting are anonymous figures. In comparison to the mood of honour expressed in David's work, exalting the notion of "dying for the nation", Goya emphasises the absurdity and theatricality of this death. The only light source is from the soldiers' square lantern. Everything seems doomed. Only the lone artist and his vision remain to give meaning to this senseless world. Goya's vision focuses entirely and without the possibility of distraction on the horror of the subject he depicts.

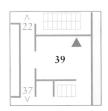

Second Floor

Basement

Francisco de Goya (1746–1828)
The Parasol, 1777
Oil on canvas, 104 x 152 cm.
Ref. no. 773

The production of cartoons for tapestries was among the earliest projects which Goya carried out at the Madrid court, and one which would occupy him for almost twenty years (1773–1791). These 63 cartoons, which have been in the Prado Museum since 1870, functioned as a sort of experimental laboratory for his later works.

The Parasol is one of the most famous of them. Here we see a seated young woman with a dog on her lap and behind her a young man (a "majo") who shades her from the sun with a green parasol. The influence of French painting on this work is obvious, and critics have cited such sources as Boucher's *Concert in the Park* or Jean Ranc's *Vertumnus and Pomona.* However, there are also major differences with French Rococo painting. Firstly, according to the art historian Michael Levey, the original element in this work is its realism, the sensation of closeness, the way the woman looks out at the spectator who enters into the reality of the scene and believes that he or she is the object of the woman's gaze. One of the pictorial challenges of the painting was how to achieve the effect of light filtering through the umbrella, resolved by Goya not so much in the French manner as in the style of Velázquez. The use of colour is not French either, but rather derives from Italian decorative painting, such as that of Corrado Giaquinto. For Goya, colour, with its clearly defined contrasts between intense and opaque, is a pictorial value in itself, an approach later taken up by modern artists. The two figures' dress is not entirely French, but rather follows Spanish contemporary fashion: the working–class young man is dressed as a "majo" while the young woman is coquettish, aristocratic and follows the French style with a fur–lined cape, a fine fichu, fan and lap–dog.

Every element in the painting has a symbolic meaning: the parasol, for example, was a fashionable object in 18th–century genre painting, appearing in outdoor rendez–vous between the woman and her lover, thus becoming symbolic of galanterie.

The composition is triangular, and there is a notable emphasis on the verticality of the elements as well as the free–standing quality of the figures as the space is not clearly defined.

Other tapestry cartoon by Goya include *The Card Players* (1778), *Boys collecting Fruit* (1778), the *Blind Man with the Guitar* (1778), *The Crockery Seller* (1789), *Harvesting* or *Summer* (1786), *The Grape Harvest* or *Autumn* (1786), *The wounded Mason* (1786), *Blind Man's Buff* (1787), *The Snow Storm* or *Winter* (1787), *The Wedding* (ca. 1792), and *The Straw Manikin* (ca. 1780).

FRANCISCO DE GOYA (1746–1828)
The Countess of Chinchón, 1800
Oil on canvas, 216 x 144 cm.
REF. NO. 7767

One of Goya's most famous portraits and an undoubted masterpiece, this painting was recently acquired by the Prado Museum. It depicts María Teresa de Borbón y Vallabriga, 15th Countess of Chinchón and Marchioness of Boadilla del Monte. She was the daughter of the Infante don Luis de Borbón, son of Philip V and Isabella Farnese and brother of Charles III. Her mother was an Aragonese aristocrat, María Teresa de Vallabriga y Rozas. The Infante's marriage to a woman of lower social rank resulted in their exile from the Madrid court.

The Countess was born in Arenas de San Pedro on 6 March 1779. Aged 18, Charles IV made it known that he intended to marry her to the all–powerful Prime Minister Manuel Godoy. This portrait was painted in 1800, three years after her marriage and the year in which her brother, Archbishop of Seville and Toledo, became a Cardinal. By the time of Godoy's fall and his removal from power, the Countess was no longer living with him as he had a well–known lover, Pepita Tudó from Malaga. María Teresa went to live with her brother in Toledo where she survived the difficult times of the French invasion and the subsequent complex political situation. She was opposed to the absolutist rule of Ferdinand VII and was therefore obliged to go into exile, first to Bordeaux in 1824 and later to Paris, where she died in 1828.

Goya depicts her here as an extremely delicate young woman, seemingly bewildered and timid, but not superficial, exquisite and elegant, her gaze one of sweet abandon, with a wreath of ears of corn on her head as a symbol of fertility, alluding to her state of pregnancy. On her right hand she wears a large ring which probably bears an image of Godoy.

The Countess exudes a feeling of calm and resolved solitude, emphasised in the painting by the lack of specific spatial references apart from the chair, as the room appears to be empty, as if the sitter was enveloped in a timelessness in which both she and the artist are complicit. The colours, light and draughtsmanship, the composition, perspective and atmosphere of the painting all come together with exceptional harmony. The result reflects Goya at his most remarkable and brilliant. He knew the Countess and admired her, coming close to her in a respectful and affectionate way, conveying the honesty and discretion which she deployed in remaining aloof from court intrigues and the scandals created by the lamentably immoral conduct of her husband. This is among the paintings which best expresses the mood of an era, while retaining its own individual artistic message.

FRANCISCO DE GOYA (1746–1828)
The clothed Maja, ca. 1797
Oil on canvas, 95 x 190 cm.
REF. NO. 741
The naked Maja, ca. 1797
Oil on canvas, 97 x 190 cm.
REF. NO. 742

Despite their fame, practically nothing is known about these two paintings. They were in the collection of Godoy from 1800 and were inventoried as such on 1 January 1808 in a list drawn up by the Grand Inquisitor, together with three other paintings of "obscene subjects". In 1815 the Secret Chamber of the Madrid Inquisition ordered, "that the said Goya should be summoned to appear before this tribunal so that he can acknowledge and declare whether he painted them, why he did so, who he painted them for and to what end", but we do not know if Goya ever actually appeared before them. It was Viardot in the mid–19th century who suggested that the paintings were possibly commissioned by the Duchess of Alba. This is not likely, but what seems probable is that the relationship between the Duchess and Goya had some influence on these paintings as the two *majas* here look like her, and she was frequently depicted in this way in Goya's drawings of this date which were collected together in the so–called *Album A*. In the *Clothed Maja* the large bow around her waist also appears in other portraits of the Duchess by the artist.

The actual commission, however, probably came from Godoy, as the paintings were in his collection and also because he is known to have liked paintings of female nudes which constituted his "secret collection" ("gavinete interior") and which included such masterpieces as Velázquez's *Rokeby Venus*. The composition of these two paintings suggests the possible influence of Titian's Venuses, but Goya departs from that model to create a new type of female nude. The pose of the *maja* is not as subtle as that of the earlier Venuses: she is not sleeping, she does not pretend to be otherwise preoccupied, nor does she look away without knowing that she is observed. Rather, she places her hands behind her head and displays reveals herself to the spectator without any sense of embarrassment. For the first time in art, an artist has depicted pubic hair. This is a real woman of flesh and blood who flaunts her sexual attractiveness in order to entice the spectator. It is her boldness rather than her clothing which may have earned her the description of *maja* by the Inquisition. The two paintings are executed with enormous freedom and strong colour contrasts which give them a palpable sensuality.

Goya
Drawings Gallery
89   88 >

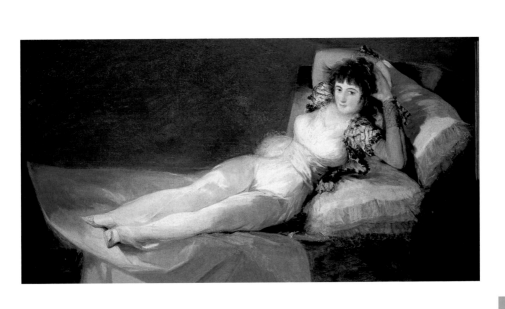

The informal parkland landscape is perhaps the greatest legacy of English painting to the visual arts in the 18th century, and can also be interpreted as a symbol of relaxed freedom in contrast to the stiff formality of the gardens of Versailles, where the control over nature might be compared to political autocracy.

THOMAS GAINSBOROUGH (1727–1788)
Isaac Henrique Sequeira, ca. 1770
Oil on canvas, 127 x 102 cm.
REF. NO. 2979

Thomas Gainsborough was among the most important English portrait and landscape painters. Born into a family of trades–people, his father funded his study of painting in London (from 1740). Gainsborough lived in Sudbury and later in Bath (from 1759). He developed a type of "conversation piece" portrait in a landscape setting. His portraits showed the influence of Van Dyck: usually life–size, they exude an elegance in line with contemporary fashion. From 1768 Gainsborough was one of the founder members of the Royal Academy, and shortly afterwards moved to London. From 1774 he became George III's preferred artist, and received numerous commissions from the aristocracy and upper middle classes. His portraits, which are extremely delicate and refined as well as enjoying the "natural elegance" of the period, have a spontaneous character that makes their depictions of the sitter extremely natural.

Here Gainsborough depicts his doctor Isaac Henrique Sequeira (1738–1816), who, as his name suggests, was a Portuguese of Jewish origin. He is depicted seated, with a book in his hands that he is not actually reading, but rather looks into the distance, perhaps thinking about some aspect of the text.

Neoclasicism or the "True Style"

The term Neo–classicism was first used in the mid–19th century. It arose almost simultaneously as a reaction against the Rococo in France, Germany and England around 1750. Its origins were intellectually complex and varied: the Enlightenment thinkers played a key role in the shift of taste, impelled by their quest for logic, clarity, simplicity and moral rectitude. A key text for the rise of Neo–classicism in art was the *Reflections on the Imitation of Greek Works in Painting and Sculpture* by Johann Joachim Winckelmann (1717–1768).

Anton Raffael Mengs (1728–1779)
Charles III, ca. 1761
Oil on canvas, 154 x 110 cm.
Ref. no. 2200

Anton Raffael Mengs was a German artist, although born in Bohemia. In Rome, he studied the work of Correggio and Raphael. Mengs was official painter to the Dresden court and knew Winckelmann, who converted him to the Neo–classical style. Charles III called him to the Spanish Court to paint the ceilings of the Royal Palace in Madrid and to execute portraits of the royal family. During his time in Spain Mengs was to prove an important influence on the younger court painters such as the Bayeu, Maella and Goya.

The present portrait was probably one of the first that he painted for Charles III following his arrival in Madrid. It is an official portrait in which the monarch appears standing in armour with the baton in his right hand. On his breast he has the orders of the Golden Fleece, the Holy Spirit and Saint Gennaro. On the table is his royal mantle of red velvet lined with ermine and ornamented with castles, lions and fleurs–de–lys. The style of the architecture and curtain are typical features of portraits of this period. Mengs's composition is extremely simple: the king is depicted three–quarter length (in contrast to French court portraits of that period which usually showed the sitter full–length). The curtain is tied up to one side and does not impinge on the picture space, the architectural element is a flat pilaster rather than a column, and finally there is no sign of an elaborate crown on the table. According to the art historian Francis Haskell, all these features show how Mengs distanced himself from French Bourbon portraits in order to create a distinct Spanish court style which showed the king as a real human being rather than a carefully dressed symbol. Here Mengs has emphasised the liveliness of the monarch's gaze and does not attempt to disguise his protuberant nose, while his mouth has the hint of a smile.

83 | 82 | 81

THE DAUPHIN'S TREASURE

The year 1712 saw the death of the Dauphin of France, son of Louis XIV and father of Philip V of Spain. His fortune, which had never been great, was divided up on the wish of Louis XIV between his three children: the lands of Meudon and Chaville went to the Duke of Burgundy as the first–born, while the treasure and objects were divided between Philip V and his brother the Duc de Berry. A few such objects were, however, auctioned to cover the Dauphin's debts. Philip V kept his share of the treasure at the Palace of La Granja and during his reign these objects were not shown to the public. Charles III had them sent to his Natural History Cabinet where they remained until the Napoleonic invasion when they were taken to Paris: on their return it was noticed that some pieces were missing. Since then, the Dauphin's Treasure has undergone further mishaps as well as various restorations up to the present day. It mainly consists of 16th and 17th–century objects and is extremely important for our knowledge of Renaissance and Baroque decorative arts at the French court.

Onyx Salt Cellar with a Gold Mermaid, First half of the 16th century
Height 17.5 cm.
REF. NO. 69

This salt cellar is French and can be related from its shape and iconography to another salt cellar held up by a gold triton which was in the collection of François I.

It consists of a shallow chalice–like vessel of oriental onyx, held up by a gold mermaid who is joined to the base by two enamelled fish tails. The mermaid is a direct reference to the fruit of the sea – salt. The base is also made of enamelled gold. As the iconography is based on a mermaid the anonymous goldsmith emphasised greenish–blue on the base in reference to the sea. The piece is embellished with 177 rubies and 2 diamonds. When described in the earliest inventories there is also reference to a dolphin located between the "legs" of the mermaid (there is a hole which might have been a fitting for it), but by 1815 this had disappeared.

© ALDEASA, 2004
Legal Deposit: M-38116-2004
I.S.B.N.: 84-8003-255-3

Published and produced by: ALDEASA
Translation: Laura Suffield
Design: Antonio Ochoa de Zabalegui
Layout: Ramón Castellanos
Photographs: Archivo Museo del Prado
Photomechanical production: Lucam
Printed by: Artes Gráficas Palermo, S.L.

Printed in Spain

This book came off the press
on 30 January 2004, in Madrid,
at the printing works of Artes Gráficas Palermo, S.L.